Economics

Economics

Volume 2

Business operations

GROLIER
EDUCATIONAL

Sherman Turnpike,
Danbury, Connecticut
06816

Published 2000 by Grolier Educational
Sherman Turnpike
Danbury, Connecticut 06816

© 2000 Brown Partworks Ltd

Set ISBN: 0-7172-9492-7
Volume ISBN: 0-7172-9483-8

Library of Congress Cataloging-in-Publication Data
Economics.
    p. cm.
    Includes index.
    Contents: v. 1 Money, banking, and finance — v. 2.
Business operations — v. 3. The citizen and the
economy — v. 4. The U.S. economy and the world —
v. 5. Economic theory — v. 6. History of economics
    ISBN 0-7172-9492-7 (set: alk. paper). — ISBN 0-7172-
9482-X (v. 1: alk. paper). — ISBN 0-7172-9483-8 (v. 2:
alk. paper). — ISBN 0-7172-9484-6 (v. 3: alk. paper). —
ISBN 0-7172-9485-4 (v. 4: alk. paper). — ISBN 0-7172-
9570-2 (v. 5: alk. paper). — ISBN 0-7172-9571-0 (v. 6:
alk. paper).
    1. Economics—Juvenile literature [1. Economics.] I.
Grolier Educational Corporation.

HB183. E26 2000
330—dc21   00-020414

For information address the publisher:
Grolier Educational, Sherman Turnpike,
Danbury, Connecticut 06816

FOR BROWN PARTWORKS LTD

Project editor:
Jane Lanigan
Editors: Tim Cooke, Julian
Flanders, Mike Janson,
Henry Russell
Editorial assistance:
Wendy Horobin,
Tim Mahoney,
Sally McEachern,
Chris Wiegand
Design: Tony Cohen,
Bradley Davis,
Matthew Greenfield
Picture research:
Helen Simm
Graphics: Mark Walker
Indexer: Kay Ollerenshaw

Project consultant: Robert
Pennington, Associate
Professor, College of
Business Administration,
University of Central Florida
Text: Nick Webber, Barry
Harrison, Nick Mathiason,
David Langridge, Dennis
Muraoka

About this book

Economics is all around us. It covers almost
every aspect of life today, from how much
money you have in your pocket to the price of
real estate, from how much tax people pay to
the causes of wars in distant lands. In today's
world it is essential to understand how to manage your money, how to save wisely, and how to
shop around for good deals. It is also important
to know the bigger picture: how financial institutions work, how wealth is created and distributed, how economics relates to politics, and
how the global economy works that ties together everyone on the planet.

   Economics places everyday financial
matters in the wider context of the sometimes
mysterious economic forces that shape our
lives, tracing the emergence of economic doc-
trines and explaining how economic systems
worked in the past and how they work now.

   Each of the six books covers a particular area of economics, from personal finance to
the world economy. Five books are split into
chapters that explore their themes in depth.
Volume 5, Economic Theory, is arranged as an A-
Z encyclopedia of shorter articles about fundamental concepts in economics and can be used
as an accessible reference when reading the
rest of the set. At the end of every chapter or
article a See Also box refers you to related articles elsewhere in the set, allowing you to further investigate topics of particular interest.

   The books contain many charts and
diagrams to explain important data clearly and
explain their significance. There are also special
boxes throughout the set that highlight particular subjects in greater detail. They might explain
how to fill out a check correctly, analyze the
theory proposed by a particular economist, or
tell a story that shows how economic theory
relates to events in our everyday lives.

   If you are not sure where to find a
subject, look it up in the set index in each
volume. The index covers all six books, so it
will help you trace topics throughout the set.
There is also a glossary at the end of the book,
which provides a brief explanation of some of
the key words and phrases that occur throughout the volumes. The extensive Further Reading
list contains many of the most recent books
about different areas of economics to allow you
to do your own research. It also features a list
of useful web sites where you can find up-to-
date information and statistics.

Contents

Business operations

An introduction to business

Businesses are more than just a part of a nation's culture—in many significant ways they define that culture and dictate the nature of many parts of our surroundings. Yet, despite their importance to society, businesses are often easier to recognize than to define.

Switch on a light, drink a cup of coffee, read a book, watch TV, buy some new clothes, get a bus to school, see a movie or snore into your pillow—if you engage in any of these activities, you will find yourself using products designed, created, and sold by businesses. Businesses not only define our material surroundings but also influence our mental world and culture. For example, Santa Claus originally wore green and white until a Coca-Cola advertising campaign depicted him in the famous red and white—now he never goes out in anything else. The Coca-Cola bottle itself is nowadays the most recognized symbol around the world. Every year, thousands of companies spend billions of dollars on direct and subliminal advertisements that we encounter every day. Business is the cornerstone of modern life.

Early businesses

A business may broadly be defined as a unit of economic organization that is designed to satisfy needs—such as food, water, and clothing—or to fulfill wants, such as holidays, movies, and CD players. As such, business is an activity that is fundamental to human social organization. Yet businesses can take on many different forms and characteristics across countries and through time. It is therefore important to understand both the evolution and the history of the modern business enterprise so that we can explain why business operates as it does today.

Businesses have not always existed in the form they do today. The development of modern business practice has its roots in the economic shifts of the medieval and early modern periods, in early trading enterprises, in the pattern of colonialism, and in the expansion of the manufacturing industry. Today's characteristic businesses, the large multi-national corporations and public enterprises, were further shaped by technological developments, taxation policies, and international conflicts of the modern era. Most historians trace the roots of modern business to the activities of the developed nations of western

LEFT: Commercial television stations are businesses that advertise a wide range of other businesses and their products.

Europe and North America because these nations created the dominant forms of business in the modern world economy.

In the typical agrarian societies of the 13th to 16th centuries in Europe business was limited mainly to local trade. The manorial

BELOW: Through advertising the logo of Coca-Cola—the quintessential U.S. corporation—has become readily recognizable all over the world, even in China.

system during this period meant that most people were engaged in agriculture. The lord of the manor would grant land to the peasantry or serfs, who would give back agricultural services in return. Due to the absence of any significant surplus, business was small-scale and consisted mainly of the bartering and exchange of goods in the marketplace. The existence of merchant guilds, chartered by the state, generally excluded large-scale trade outside particular geographical regions. The businesses that did exist were then mainly sole proprietors, trading goods or crafts in the local area.

In addition to this small-scale business activity there existed chartered companies, which were engaged in trade with foreign countries. Such companies were granted charters by governments, which usually gave monopolistic trade rights for a defined geographical area. Every regulated company of this type was a corporation of merchants, all of whom traded on their own account but were subjected to a rigid set of common rules, usually defined to stabilize prices and profits. One of the earliest examples of a chartered company was the Merchant Adventurers of England, who were granted a charter in 1407 to export cloth, first to the Netherlands and later to northwest Germany. Chartered companies were also popular in France and the Netherlands from the 16th century onward.

Colonial expansion

It was in this area of foreign trade that the development of business was most advanced in the preindustrial era. While companies were chartered for trade, they were also at the forefront of colonialism. The London Company, the Plymouth Company, and the Massachusetts Bay Company were directly

involved in the settlement of colonists in North America. England, France and the Netherlands each formed their own East India Company, and these businesses were involved in violent battles that are as much a part of colonial as of trading history. Given the risky and expensive nature of their enterprises, these companies began to operate on a joint-stock basis—that is, they borrowed money from investors who would share in any resulting profits. This enabled the capital investment necessary for such undertakings to be drawn from a much wider area. Moreover, with a government charter such investors were liable only for the amount they invested rather than for the full losses a company might incur—this is known today as "limited

ABOVE: Although the earliest recorded human trade was barter, by the 15th century Europe had become a continent of merchants who parted with their wares for money rather than other commodities.

LEFT: As maritime and overland lines of communication improved, foreign trade increased, bringing to Europe for the first time a wide range of new and exotic products from Africa and Asia.

liability." However, following the Bubble Act of 1720 in the United Kingdom, joint-stock companies declined in popularity because of the new reality of full liability for all investors.

In order to meet the need for larger amounts of capital, limited partnerships then became popular. A limited partnership is an arrangement by which only some of the partners are fully liable for the losses of the business. Limited partnerships were common in Europe and the United States in the 18th and early 19th centuries. The growth of enterprises and the demand for greater amounts of capital led gradually to the acceptance of the corporate form from the mid-19th century. It became the most important form of business organization in the modern world.

A series of socioeconomic developments took place that were crucial for the emergence of modern business:
● The development of a laboring class resulting from the breakup of the manorial system created a group of people who were dependent for their survival on the availability of labor rather than land. This process was affected too by population growth.
● Capital was freed up for investment. For example, the English navigator Sir Francis Drake (1540-96) started the Levant Company using as capital the gold and silver bullion he had acquired by sacking Spanish galleons.
● A system of finance was gradually constructed. It included the extension of credit, the acceptance of loans with interest as a general practice, and the establishment of banks. They were all vital in providing the means for small businesses to expand into larger enter-

ABOVE: The first New York building of the Edison Electric Light Company, a great U.S. private firm.

BELOW: The Golden Hind, the most famous of the ships commanded by Sir Francis Drake.

prises. This process was cemented further with the establishment of the Bank of England in 1694.
● The "entrepreneur" appeared as a calculated risk-taker, one who invests his or her own and others' money in new enterprises and in the expansion of existing ones. An entrepreneurial spirit emerged in England and Europe from the 16th century and in the United States from the late 18th century.
● The development of a wage system and population growth helped create a large, mobile workforce in many developing countries. Workers were increasingly subjected to a new industrial discipline, which often entailed long periods of work, typically 12 to 14 hours a day, at a relentless pace because of mechanization.
● The Industrial Revolution was crucial for the development of modern business, in particular the start of the factory system. The factory system was designed by the Englishman Richard Arkwright (1732-92) at the end of the 18th century and was widely adopted. America's first factory was the Boston Manufacturing Company, opened in 1814.
● The rigors of labor were later extended after the birth of what became known as scientific management. Such management techniques—largely developed by U.S. businessman and engineer F.W. Taylor (1856-1915)—were based on the theory that a business was most efficient if all labor was specialized, divided into a range of simple tasks, and practiced through manufacturing using conveyor belts.

F.W. Taylor—the original time-and-motion man

Known as the father of scientific management, U.S. inventor and engineer Frederick Winslow Taylor was born in Philadelphia, Pennsylvania, on March 20, 1856. He passed the entrance examinations for Harvard University but never took up his place there because of failing eyesight. Instead, he became an apprentice patternmaker and machinist at the Enterprise Hydraulic Works in his native city. In 1878 he moved to the Midvale Steel Company, where he began as a machine shop laborer but rose rapidly to become, in quick succession, shop clerk, machinist, gang boss, foreman, maintenance foreman, head of the drawing office, and chief engineer.

In 1881—the same year in which, incidentally, he and a tennis partner won the U.S. National Doubles Championship—Taylor introduced time study at the Midvale plant. The project was so successful that it was soon taken up by progressive firms elsewhere in the U.S. and across the world.

The idea that formed the basis of Taylor's management theories was that production efficiency in a factory or shop could be improved by closely observing individual workers and using the information thereby obtained to eliminate wasted time and motion from their operation practices. Although time-and-motion studies provoked opposition and resentment when carried to extremes, their precepts were most helpful in rationalizing production, and their effect on techniques of mass production was immense.

Frederick Taylor published many books, the most important of which was *The Principles of Scientific Management* (1911). He died in Philadelphia on March 21, 1915.

The rise of labor unions

However, alongside these developments, the struggle between capital and labor was taking shape, and it led directly to the organization of labor or trade unions. In Europe trade unions formed the bedrock of working-class defiance against their employers: the development of such political bodies created a natural constituency for socialism and went hand in hand with the growth of labor parties. Some of the conflicts caused by these left-wing stirrings led to bloody revolutions and violent countermeasures by governments. In the United States unions such as the Knights of St. Crispin, the American Federation of Labor (AFL), and the Congress of Industrial Organizations (CIO) were less radical than some of their European counterparts, concentrating on securing better wages, hours, and working conditions but never challenging the established social order. Although strongly resisted at first by entrepreneurs and governments alike, organized labor has since become an acceptable and—as evidenced in the U.S. Wagner Act of 1935—an important consideration in the growth and structure of modern business.

So by the start of the 20th century the corporate form of business had evolved, mitigated to some degree by the demands of an organized labor force. The growth of these corporations has been pivotal in the development of the modern business structure. New technologies in the manufacturing industry demanded larger-scale businesses to cope. Such developments as the internal combustion engine meant that businesses needed larger amounts of capital over longer terms than ever before. Such necessities as research departments in the chemical industry could not be funded by small firms. In the late 19th century the United States became the largest manufacturing country in the world, and it was dominated by big business. As President Calvin Coolidge famously said, "America's business is business."

The growth of big business

The need to protect businesses from the potentially ruinous effects of competition led to the development of gentlemen's agreements and cartels. These cartels usually involved price-fixing and the designation of geographical areas in which each company could trade monopolistically. In 1926 a steel cartel was formed involving companies from

BELOW: In the 19th century the development of large workforces led to the growth of the labor movement, as employees united against possible exploitation and in search of a better deal.

Belgium, France, Germany, and Luxembourg. However, such cartels often broke down, since the desire of management to increase their own firm's sales remained stronger than the need to cooperate when it came to a choice between the two options. The formation of huge trusts was seen as a better alternative. This meant that large companies consolidated all firms in an entire industry to form monopolies. This was the policy of the Standard Oil Company. Following state legislation to outlaw such corporate behavior, holding companies were formed as a way around this obstacle. As J.D. Rockefeller (1839-1937)—for many years part-owner of Standard Oil—said, "The day of combination is here to stay."

The earliest multinationals

Another part of this trend of big business was the development of multinational firms. The U.S. sewing machine company Singer built its first overseas factory in Glasgow, Scotland, in 1867. As such, it became the first true multinational, producing the same manufactured item in the same form and with the same name in different parts of the world. The modern multinational became possible through the improvement in transportation

ABOVE: Industrial growth continued into the 20th century. In 1863 this hat-making firm employed only 20 people; by 1909, when this photograph was taken, more than 700 skilled men and women were employed at the factory in Manchester, England.

LEFT: The cover of this magazine expresses some of the widely held misgivings about the excessive power and dehumanizing influence of the U.S. dollar, which is here depicted as a vulture.

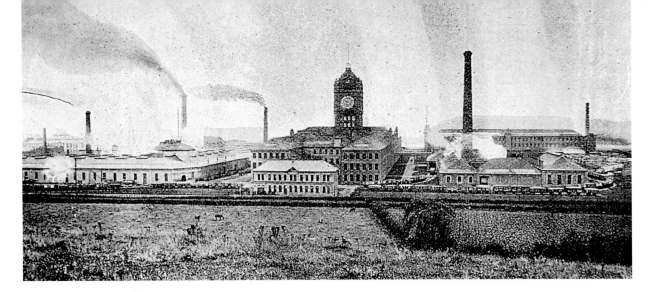

and communication that occurred in the 20th century and the development of mass markets. It was also encouraged by the decision of various nations to tax imported goods—a policy known as protectionism—and by the development of trading blocs such as the European Free Trade Association (EFTA) and, more recently, the European Community (EC).

The construction of large corporations in technologically advanced industries necessitated the reform of the internal organization of businesses. This shift was epitomized in the development of organizational theory, advanced by philosophers such as Max Weber and Henri Fayol. In particular, as a result of the increasingly important economic role of the state, the growing role of banks in business (finance capitalism), the enhanced importance of labor unions, and the greater size and complexity of businesses, a professional managerial class emerged. Due to the size and specialized knowledge of business, it was no longer possible for the stockholders to meet and formulate policy. The managerial revolution entailed the complex bureaucratic division of business organization. Separate departments were created for sales, accountancy, public relations, advertising, product development, and research. They were staffed by the new white-collar workers, above whom were supervisors and managers who made decisions within their own areas of authority. The days of the heroic entrepreneur, singlehandedly and sometimes recklessly making decisions that determined the fate of huge businesses and hundreds of jobs, were over. Decision-making increasingly became the responsibility of committees in which each specialized manager would have some input but no overall control.

After World War II the dominant form of business became the large corporation. It was often international and had specialized departments with managers reporting to a central committee that ran the company on behalf of the stockholders. The postwar period witnessed the acceleration and accentuation of big business, with a mass of mergers and the growth of multinationals. Also, however, the experience of the World War II led—especially in Europe—to an unprecedentedly high level of state intervention and the growth of the public sector. In the United Kingdom and France, for example, the state nationalized such industries as coal-mining and transportation and ran them as public corporations on similar lines to large

ABOVE: By opening this sewing machine factory in Glasgow, Scotland, the U.S. firm Singer became the first true multinational.

BELOW: The growth of the railroad system made an important contribution to the U.S. economy in the 19th century.

private enterprises. Thus, modern forms of business emerged from complex economic shifts that have shaped almost every aspect of the modern Western—and even world—experience.

Modern business categories

Modern businesses appear in a vast range of shapes and sizes—they are organized in many different ways and operate on many different principles. They are also described differently by different commentators—business students, governments and their agencies, financial analysts, and businessmen themselves have contributed to the development of a complex descriptive categorization of businesses. These categorizations take account of factors such as the ownership, the size of the business, the objectives, the type of output of the business, and the internal structure of the business, as well as other factors.

Categorization by profit

One of the main methods of categorizing a business is according to whether it makes or intends to make a profit (*see* page 28, How a business works). Firms can be divided into profit-making businesses, state-funded businesses, and charities.

Profit-making businesses usually operate in the private sector and consist of limited companies, partnerships, sole proprietors, and others. Most businesses in the United States fall into the private sector, with well-known examples being McDonald's, the Ford Motor Co., and Microsoft. Smaller businesses of this type include the shops in the local mall, the plumber, and the door-to-door salesman.

Charities are businesses that depend on private donations and can therefore be viewed as part of the private sector. Despite having different aims, they are often organized and function in ways similar to profit-making businesses. The main distinction is that charities do not make profits, and their expenditure should match their income over a given period of time. An example of a charity is the International Red Cross, which is funded by donations and grants, and which sends qualified health workers to various war zones and natural disaster areas throughout the world.

State-funded businesses are in the public sector and consist of nationalized industries, local government, the army, and the civil service. Businesses in the public sector are wholly or partly owned by the state and are controlled through a public authority. The state funds such organizations by the levying of taxes on the profits of private business, on the income of employees, and on the expenditures of consumers. Any profits made by

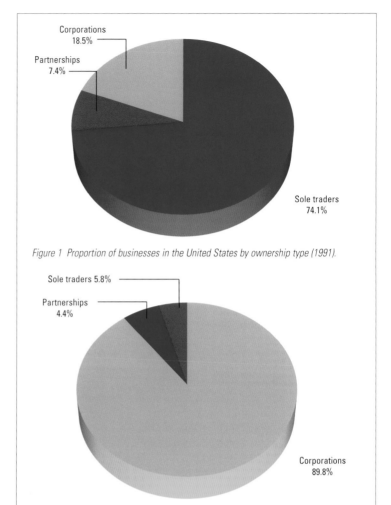

Figure 1 *Proportion of businesses in the United States by ownership type (1991).*

Figure 2 *Proportion of business receipts in the United States by ownership type (1991).*

such organizations are plowed back into government funds. Businesses are placed under public ownership so that the service or product they supply is provided through a state monopoly. Typically, such businesses include the utilities (electricity, water, etc.), broadcasting, and transportation. In some countries businesses are nationalized for ideological reasons, most commonly to achieve the socialist objective of public ownership of the means of production as a way to a fairer society. Such nationalized industries typically include railroads, coal-mining, and banking. Alternatively, the state may wish to control businesses for strategic reasons—it will retain control of armaments and aircraft manufacture, for example, because a private firm in charge of these industries would acquire too much political power.

In Europe most societies are organized as "mixed" economies, that is, with a moderate public sector. In the United Kingdom and France after World War II the state assumed control of private businesses in coal-mining, the railways, utility provision, banks, and

LEFT: Ford has such a firmly established international identity and presence that many people do not fully realize that it is a U.S. rather than a domestic company. This assembly line is in Ontario, Canada.

insurance companies. In communist societies, such as the former Soviet Union, all business was owned by the state. In many newly independent and less-developed countries there is also a very large public enterprise sector. In the United States, however, private companies are generally allowed to provide most of the above-named services subject to strict legal regulations. The United States has few public enterprises, the most significant being the Tennessee Valley Authority—established 1933—and the U.S. postal system.

Categorization by function

Some commentators categorize businesses according to their function. Under this method there are four categories of firm: primary, secondary, tertiary, and quaternary.

The businesses belonging to the primary sector are often termed "extractive businesses" because they are concerned with the removal of natural resources from the environment. Natural resources may be classified either as renewable (e.g., fish) or nonrenewable (e.g., oil and coal). Such businesses depend heavily on the availability of natural resources in the appropriate area. For example, Texas is oil-rich, and numerous businesses in the state have thrived following the discovery of oil reserves under their land. Many of the earth's precious natural resources are concentrated in certain countries: one-quarter of the world's oil is found in Saudi Arabia; almost one-third of the world's gold is found in South Africa.

Disputes over the ownership of natural resources have led—and continue to lead—to violent political confrontations. The often brutal implementation of European colonialism followed the routes of the trade in precious spices in the East Indies and the gold trails across Mexico and in South Africa. More recently, Iraq's attempt to annex oil-rich Kuwait led to the 1991 Gulf War. On a smaller scale

there have been many violent disputes between fishermen of one nationality over the right to fish in another country's waters. A 1999 European Union regulation allowing Spanish boats to fish in waters previously used only by British vessels has resulted in conflict between the two countries' fishermen over rights of ownership of this natural resource.

However, the economic success of Japan, for example, has been achieved despite the fact that the country has very few natural

BELOW: The Tennessee Valley Authority (TVA) is one of the United States' few public companies. The TVA dam shown here under construction was part of the 1930s New Deal.

resources of its own. This is due to the great competitiveness of its businesses engaged in secondary industry. Secondary industry, or manufacturing industry, converts the output from primary industry and puts it to other uses. Traditionally, manufacturing businesses flourish where labor costs are low, or where there is a ready availability of people with relevant skills. Hence Japan in the late 1980s remarkably began to dominate the international car industry through the success of such firms as Honda, Nissan, and Toyota. The same type of effect may be seen in India and Taiwan, which have become major suppliers of electrical goods and clothes.

The historical geography of secondary industry follows an interesting pattern. Britain underwent the world's first Industrial Revolution from the mid-18th century to the late 19th century for a number of complex reasons. The Revolution was founded on the dramatic expansion of secondary industry and the proliferation of manufactured goods. However, the ideal conditions for the prosperity of manufacturing businesses were gradually undermined as a result of the organization of labor and through various political developments. Britain's economy has steadily—and occasionally dramatically—shifted toward the tertiary sector. This shift is also

ABOVE: Coal strip mining near Caldwell, Ohio. Coal is a valuable natural resource that is nonrenewable— when supplies are exhausted, there is no way of replenishing them.

LEFT: Inspectors examining Toyota cars as they come off the assembly line at Miyazaki, Japan. With Honda and Nissan, Toyota is one of the big three Japanese automobile manufacturers.

partly due to competition from lower wages paid to workers in countries such as India, South Korea, and Taiwan.

Businesses engaged in tertiary industry are those that use the products of secondary industry to provide services. Such businesses provide financial, health, and educational services, and many others. It is the expansion of tertiary industries that has sustained economic growth in the United States, Europe, Canada, and Australia.

Lastly, the quaternary sector of the economy is very small and consists solely of businesses that provide indirect services such as setting standards and offering advice. This sector is composed typically of watchdogs, institutes, and government advisory bodies.

Types of ownership

In addition to the broad categories of enterprise outlined above, businesses may also be defined and categorized according to types of ownership and more specific legal stipulations. As business and the laws governing business have evolved, the types of business have changed. Today, there are three major types of ownership in the private sector—sole

ABOVE: An electronics factory in Bangalore, India, one of the developing countries in which multinationals can achieve high levels of production with low overheads and labor costs.

LEFT: Healthcare is one of the most important examples of a tertiary industry.

proprietor, partnership, and corporation—and each is distinguished by the legal responsibilities of its owner or owners. In addition to these three there are numerous other specific business forms that are important to the modern economy. They include multinational corporations, subsidiaries, shells, parents, joint ventures, public corporations, franchises, and cooperatives.

Sole proprietors

The most basic type of ownership is the sole proprietor. It is the simplest and most common form of business enterprise, in which one person sets up a business and starts trading. Although such businesspeople may employ others, they are the sole owners. Sole proprietors are entrepreneurs, the risk takers of the business world. At worst, sole proprietors are personally liable for all debts incurred by the business, which can mean the forced sale of possessions, the repossession of a home, and civil (or criminal) court proceedings. At best, successful sole proprietors expand their businesses into large companies. For example, English businessman Sir Richard Branson started his Virgin company as a 16-year-old selling records by mail order. Today Virgin is a giant empire, with large stakes in the music, media, soft drinks, Internet, airline, and railway industries. More commonly, although sole proprietors enjoy complete freedom of decisions, they find it difficult to leave the business for such things as vacations—if a householder has a burst pipe while his or her regular plumber is on vacation, he or she is not going to wait for the plumber's return to have it fixed but will contact a competitor.

Partnerships

The second type of ownership is known as partnership, in which the business is owned by between two and 20 partners. Typically, a deed of partnership is drawn up that records such things as how much each partner has contributed toward the business, each partner's responsibilities, the distribution of profits, and the agreed methods for reducing, expanding, or dissolving the partnership. Partnerships exist for people of the same trade or profession—for example, a group of veterinarians may form a partnership, allowing the practice to offer 24-hour service. Alternatively, partnerships may form across trades and professions—where, for instance, a plumber, bricklayer, carpenter, and plasterer may join forces to build houses—and across specialties—in which, say, lawyers specializing in different types of law may join forces to offer a comprehensive range of legal services to a local population. Partnerships involve collective decision making—they may lead to

better decisions or, alternatively, to internal conflict and inefficiency. As with sole proprietors, the partners in a firm are also liable for the debts incurred by the partnership.

Corporations

The third type of business is the corporation, the most important form of business organization. It is a specific legal form of organization, chartered by the state for the purpose of conducting a business, which is owned by two or more shareholders. As contrasted with the other two major forms of business ownership, the corporation is distinguished by several characteristics that make it a more flexible instrument for large-scale economic activity.

The first characteristic is limited liability for the shareholders. After the shareholders have bought their shares, they are not liable for any further loss; nor are the shareholders responsible for any debts that the business may incur. Thus, if the company makes a loss, and its creditors (the people to whom the

ABOVE: Sir Richard Branson, the founder of Virgin, grew his company from a record retailer into one of the world's leading multinationals, which includes investment firms and an airline.

business owes money) claim their money, the business is obliged by law to pay only from the value that exists within the business itself. Only in rare circumstances can the personal wealth of the directors or shareholders be called on.

This system is flexible in that the rights in the enterprise may be transferred readily from one investor to another without reconstituting the organization under law.

Second, the corporation is seen as having a distinct legal personality. The corporation is regarded as a fictive "person"—the business is separate from its owners, unlike the situation that obtains with a partnership or a sole proprietorship—and thus may sue and be sued, make contracts, and hold property in a common name.

Third, the corporation may have an indefinite duration—this is to say that the life of the corporation may extend beyond the participation of any of its incorporators.

Corporations may be privately or publicly held. Most small corporations are privately held—the stock of the corporation is held by a relatively small number of private individuals and is not traded on a stock market. A publicly held corporation, on the other hand, is one that has decided to "go public," in which case it will issue shares of its stock to the general public. Once the stock of a company has been issued, it can be traded on a stock exchange. Both privately held and publicly held corporations follow the same general structural pattern; the main distinction is this issue of stock ownership.

Limited liability

Some partnerships expand by becoming public companies and issuing shares on the stock exchange, a move that provides the benefits of limited liability for the partners and an injection of capital. However, it also means that the company can then be taken over if someone acquires more than 50 percent of the shareholding in the business, whereas this can never happen to a privately held company.

Therefore a crucial factor in distinguishing between types of business and systems of ownership is the concept of liability. For a sole proprietor personal liability is total; for a shareholder of a public corporation liability is limited only to the investment made and not to any personal assets.

The acceptance and widespread implementation of this principle of limited liability by business and governments was a vital factor in the development of large-scale industry. Following a speculative panic in England 1720 joint-stock enterprises experienced a crisis of capital availability. Investors were understandably reluctant to commit large sums to a

business if the failure of that business might mean personal liability and the loss of private fortunes. To meet the need for larger amounts of capital in business, limited partnerships became increasingly popular.

A limited partnership is an arrangement identical to a normal partnership apart from the fact that some—but not all—partners arrange to be liable only for the amounts invested by them in the business. Limited partnerships were common both in Europe and the United States in the 18th and early 19th centuries.

Gradually, however, the idea of the corporate system—limited liability for all owners—took root. Between 1844 and 1862 many full joint-stock companies were created with limited liability for all shareholders. The formation of corporate enterprises was also made simpler in France and Germany by legal reforms during the 1860s and 1870s. From this time on, the limited liability company was firm-

ABOVE: The electronic board above the floor of the New York Stock Exchange shows the final numbers after the Dow Jones Industrial Average closed above 10,000 for the first time on March 29, 1999.

ly established as the most important and successful form of commercial association in modern economies.

Access to finance

Access to finance is crucial to the development of modern big business. In any business capital is required for such things as land, buildings, and machinery. Finance is needed to establish, maintain, and expand the business.

A major disadvantage for a sole proprietor is the lack of access to financial capital. The sole proprietor depends on the finance that he or she can initially raise because banks are unlikely to lend more than a modest sum to any such concern without security. This presents a major obstacle to the expansion of the business and even to its very survival if a large injection of capital is required for modernization. Moreover, a lack of access to finance may make it difficult for a sole proprietor to survive a short-term setback, even if in the long term the prospects for the firm are good. Partnerships face similar problems, although they are reduced to some extent if a large number of partners invest in the business; however, their ability to borrow is still restricted to comparatively small amounts.

By contrast, because investors have only a limited liability, corporations are much more successful in accessing finance. Thus a share issue—the sale of shares in a corporation—is an effective way of increasing capital. Corporations are larger than small firms, and hence their borrowing power is much greater. The use of franchise agreements is another useful way of expanding a business without increasing personal borrowing (*see* The power of the franchise, page 22).

Lack of access to finance was one of the main obstacles faced by British entrepreneur Anita Roddick when she attempted to start The Body Shop in 1976. She solved the initial problem of funding her first shop by gaining some financial backing (the equivalent of around $8,000) from an acquaintance who owned a garage. The two of them thus effectively formed a private limited liability company and agreed under the terms of formation that they wouldshare any future profits. Anita Roddick was then able to open more shops by issuing franchises. Eventually, The Body Shop became a public corporation, with the public sale of shares on the stock exchange. This was so that the company could gain access to finance and further expand its operations without increasing the personal borrowing and indebtedness

BELOW: Anita Roddick, the English businesswoman who opened her first Body Shop with private backing in 1976. The chain is now an international market leader.

LEFT: A camera operator filming for ABC in Minneapolis, Minnesota. ABC has grown enormously as it has changed ownership over the years.

of Anita Roddick herself. Today, The Body Shop has more than one thousand shops in nearly fifty different countries, and the two original owners are multimillionaires.

Multinational corporations—which are also known as transnational corporations—are firms that are registered and operate in several different countries at the same time. Ordinarily, a multinational corporation has its headquarters in one country and operates wholly or partly owned subsidiaries in other countries. Essentially, multinationals benefit from economies of scale and the resulting power of monopoly—they are the main reasons for their existence. Technical expertise and marketing strategies can commonly be transferred across national borders. The cost of developing new products can be recouped much more quickly by trading in several different countries. Also, by establishing offices or manufacturing plants in other countries, a multinational often avoids taxation on imported goods. This is evident in the numerous U.S. and Japanese automobile manufacturing plants that have been established throughout Europe. The fast food chain McDonald's, the sportswear manufacturer Nike, and the soft drink company Coca-Cola are other classic examples of large multinational corporations. Multinationals are often denounced as agents of a new colonialism (neoimperialism), constituting an economic, cultural, and political means of foreign domination. Developing countries are seen as particularly vulnerable to this form of oppression; others argue that countries gain more than they lose from the presence of foreign firms.

Subsidiaries, shells, parents

A subsidiary is a company wholly controled by another. Subsidiaries are usually companies that were formerly independent but have since been bought out by larger companies. The American Broadcasting Company (ABC) is an example of a company that first owned subsidiaries before itself becoming a subsidiary of another company, which in turn become a subsidiary of a third corporation. In 1955 ABC entered the phonograph record business with the purchase of a subsidiary and, over the years, developed such labels as ABC, Westminster, Dot, and Impulse. In 1985 ABC was purchased by Capital Cities Communications, Inc., thereby itself becoming a subsidiary. In 1995-96 Capital Cities/ABC Inc. became a subsidiary of the Walt Disney Company for $19 billion.

Shells and parents

Distinct from a subsidiary is a shell company or corporation, which is a business that exists without assets or independent operations. Such a business is often set up so that another business can conduct various dealings through it.

A parent or holding company is a corporation that effectively controls one or more other companies through ownership of the requisite amount of voting stock in those companies. While it is usually the case that the parent company owns more than 50 percent of the stock in the subsidiary, there are some exceptions: for example, if the ownership of the remaining shares is sufficiently

diffuse, even though aggregating to a majority, then the parent company can effectively control the smaller company as a subsidiary. A corporation that exists solely for this purpose is known as a holding company, while one that also engages in a business of its own is known as a holding-operating company. The use of a holding company is often preferred for two main reasons: first, because it is legally simpler and less costly to establish a parent company than to organize a merger or consolidation of existing firms; second, by retaining at least the name and some of the personnel of the subsidiary, the holding company benefits from the goodwill and reputation that the subsidiary has established (the brand), and yet its liability is limited to the proportion of the subsidiary's stock that it owns.

With a wide range of interests in petroleum operations, chemical products, and retailing, the Mobil Corporation is one of the largest holding or parent companies in the United States. The Mobil Corporation was formed in 1976 to act as a pure holding company in the merger of two separate corporations, Mobil Oil and Marcor Inc. Today, the Mobil Corporation undertakes drilling operations in many parts of the world, with major produc-

tion in the Gulf of Mexico, California, the North Sea, and Saudi Arabia, as well as along the U.S. Atlantic seaboard and on the Alaskan North Slope.

Joint-venture companies

A joint-venture company is a separate limited liability company formed and owned by two or more preexistent limited liability companies. Companies form joint ventures to work on a particular project or projects in a specific market or markets. The corporations that have undertaken the new venture agree to share its profits and losses according to the size of their initial investments. Such joint-venture companies were popular from the 17th century in foreign trade in the form of such concerns as the Muscovy Company and the British East India Company.

State-controlled companies

In many countries the state has become the majority shareholder in some corporations, forming public corporations. A public corporation is created by a government, which defines its powers, management structure, and its relationship with government bodies. The capital requirements of a state-controlled company are met by the national treasury, but it is generally supposed to meet its current expenses from normal commercial operations. The public corporation is distinct from the state company, which is simply an ordinary joint-stock company whose shares are owned wholly or partly by the state. Advantages for public corporations include the ability to plan in the longer term since the finance of the state is sufficient to protect it from short-term adversity. This system has been of great benefit to SNCF, the French rail network, which, because of large-scale capital investment since the end of World War II in 1945, has the fastest passenger trains in the world. Also, for social reasons public corporations may receive state subsidies or enjoy additional protection that is not available to competitors. However, in recent years public corporations have come to be widely—and not always unfairly—regarded as inefficient bodies that are no more than drains on the public purse.

One example of a highly successful public corporation is the French automobile giant Renault, which is controlled by the French government. The company was started by the Renault brothers and has been trading since 1899. After World War II the Renault facilities that had not been destroyed were confiscated by the French government, which set up the state-controlled Régie Nationale des Usines Renault in 1945. The company then concentrated on the construction of popular, inexpensive family cars, a market in which it

ABOVE: Large oil corporations, perhaps with a wide range of petroleum operations, drilling, and retailing interests, may find it simpler and less costly to operate as as a holding company.

LEFT: Government investment enabled SNCF, the French national railroad system, to develop the TGV, the world's fastest passenger train.

quickly became one of the world leaders. Between 1979 and 1987 Renault was heavily involved in the North American car industry, holding controlling interests in the American Motors Corporation and then in Mack Trucks Inc.; Renault also owned the French-based heavy-truck subsidiary Citröen. In 1994 the French government partially privatized Renault, selling off shares until it retained no more than a 50.1 percent—but still controlling, therefore—stake in the company.

The power of the franchise

A franchise is commonly a business idea or brand that the franchise owner allows someone else—the franchisee—to use in return for a fee. This fee can consist of the compulsory purchase of the products for sale from the franchise holder, or it may take the form of an initial outlay and a percentage of all sales value thereafter. In return, the franchise owner promises not to open a similar business in a defined area around the franchisee's premises. This system is popular because the franchisee is allowed to trade under the banner of an established brand. This limits the risk of failure and increases the prospects of access to finance from a bank or other lending institution. In turn, the franchise holder is able to expand the business without further capital outlay and without incurring further liabilities.

One of the most famous franchise holders is Harland Sanders, founder of the Kentucky Fried Chicken fast food chain. Sanders was born in 1890, in Shelbyville, Kentucky, and left school in the seventh grade. In 1929 he opened Sanders Café at a service station in Corbin, Kentucky. The café was such a great success that in 1935 Sanders received his honorary colonel's title from the governor of Kentucky. In 1939 Colonel Sanders perfected his recipe for "finger lickin' good chicken" and, after selling his original restaurant, took to the road with his new recipe. Despite initial apathy, by 1964 there were more than 600 Kentucky Fried Chicken franchises in the United States and Canada, and Sanders himself was earning $300,000 a year. In the same year Sanders sold most of his fast-food empire for $2 million, a lifetime salary of $40,000 per annum, and a seat on the board of executives. The company continued to grow, and by 1971 there were 3,500 franchises worldwide and $700 million a year in business. Sanders remained actively involved in the company and even appeared in advertisements despite being more than 80 years old.

The cooperative

The cooperative was originally devised in the 19th century in England as an idealistic alternative to conventional capitalism. A cooperative is a group of people who choose to form a business together, with all the participants sharing the profits of the collective endeavor. The executives and managers are accountable ultimately to the enterprise members—employees and those who use the business—rather than to external owners of stock.

BELOW: In the United Kingdom cooperative ownership ensured the survival of motorcycle manufacturers that might otherwise have gone bankrupt or been swallowed up by larger firms.

In most countries cooperatives are governed by different laws from those that regulate ordinary business associations. The cooperative is particularly associated with offering credit facilities. The three principal types of cooperative are the retail or consumer cooperative, the producer cooperative, and the cooperative joint venture. Most retail cooperatives are limited liability companies that sell essential food and clothes through a retail outlet. Their profits are shared among the members of the cooperative according to the amount of money they have spent over a given period.

Producer or worker cooperatives are owned by the workforce, who share the work, the decision-making, and ultimately the profits. The British motorcycle manufacturers Triumph and Norton are examples of producer cooperatives.

Cooperative joint ventures are formed when individual businesses combine for a specific purpose. In France, for example, wine makers from a particular region join forces to produce, market, and sell their wine. Such initiatives provide economies of scale in capital outlay (*see* How a business works, page 28; Competition, expansion and growth, page 62) and can protect producers from the adverse financial repercussions of short-term, seasonal crop failure.

Businesses in combination

The forms of business are many and diverse. In addition to the types described above, individual businesses may combine to create new business forms. The two principal combinations are the syndicate and the cartel.

A syndicate is a group of businesses or individuals that combine to carry out a particular transaction for their mutual benefit. Syndicates are commonly formed when companies combine to buy up shares in another corporation or to complete a single project. It was one such syndicate that created the Alaska pipeline.

Similarly but more controversially, a cartel is a group of businesses that combine in order to limit competition and fix prices. In the West the cartel as a business form is most dominant in Germany, a situation that developed largely as a response to the demands made on the national economy during World War II (1939-45). Members of a cartel remain as separate businesses but agree to engage in mutually beneficial common policies. The cartel effectively puts the participant businesses in a monopolistic position. They benefit from this by fixing prices, by allocating sales quotas and discrete geographical areas in which each can trade, and by combining in productive activities. Thus the establishment of a cartel may protect the businesses from dangerous com-

ABOVE: From small beginnings just before World War II Colonel Sanders' Kentucky Fried Chicken franchise grew steadily and spread to many parts of the globe. This branch is in St. Pamphile, Quebec, Canada.

petition and low prices. However, from a consumer perspective cartels logically keep prices high. Moreover, the formation of cartels often leads to industry stagnation—this is because there is no longer any need for technological development, and new competitors do not stand a chance of success. While the laws of different countries concerning cartels differ, there has been a general move in most modern states to restrict the use of cartels and to break up existing combinations.

Business organization

With the growth of big business came the development of organization within the business. Such organization includes the formal establishment of goals, the adoption of a managerial system, the development of specialized and separate departments, the creation of chains of command, and the fostering of specific organizational cultures. It should be noted that structure is not an issue until firms reach a certain size—many small firms have little or no discernible corporate shape.

The rise of management

The separation of ownership from control led naturally to the development of a managerial class. The owners of the business corporation have limited control over the company. In the modern corporation each share of stock comes with the right to cast one vote in the election of members of the board of directors. In exceptional circumstances some shares may not even carry voting rights. At the obligatory annual general meeting of any company shareholders elect directors, make decisions about dividends—whether to distribute them,

and if so, how much they will be—vote on any change to the form of the corporation, and appoint professional accountants to audit the company's books.

It is the board of directors that represents the final authority on corporate decisions. The board of directors represents shareholders, sets corporate policy, and distributes dividends. Commonly there are two types of director. The first is an employee of the company, a manager involved in the day-to-day running of the company's operations, the most important of whom is the chief executive officer (CEO). The second type is the nonexecutive director, coming from outside the company as a banker or supplier, and representing the interests of the shareholders. The board of directors in turn selects and hires senior managers to help it run the company from day to day.

Within the company there are various committees—consisting mainly of senior management—that are responsible for all the activities of the company. Typically, the senior management committee will make decisions about global corporate strategy, government relations, and the external economic environment. The global corporate strategy can be divided into the mission of the company, the objectives or goals of the company, and the strategies of the company. The mission is the master strategy, a vision of the ultimate goals of the organization. It is often summed up in a mission statement—for example, a leisure center may have the mission to be the best provider of recreational activities in a given region. A company's objectives are specific intentions measured in a certain time frame—for example, it may aim to have a 20 percent

LEFT: This great pipeline across Alaska was built by a syndicate of oil-producing firms acting in concert to their mutual advantage.

market share in five years. The strategies are the means by which these ends can be reached; the senior executives will decide what actions to take and how resources should be allocated to make them possible.

The senior management team also defines the culture of the organization. It varies according to both the management structure—which may be hierarchical, egalitarian, centralized, or devolved—and the emphasis, which may be either person- or task-centered. The senior management is also principally responsible for the structure of the company, which may vary according to technology (new communication systems have allowed multinationals to become more centralized), size, strategy, environment, internal culture, and the need to adapt to the market. As a broad general rule, firms in the United States stress particularly the finance and marketing functions, whereas German firms tend to emphasize the importance of production.

There are six principal forms of business structure today, although it should be noted that there are yet more company structures, and new ones are developing all the time. The main ones at present are as follows:

● The functional business structure is currently the most common. Within this structure employees perform related specialized tasks and are grouped together under a single management structure. Typical groupings or departments are finance, marketing, production, and personnel.

● The divisional form of structure is operated by large corporations and multinationals. Each division is self-contained and is operated as a profit center, but each is directed by central headquarters. Divisions can be arranged geographically, as is the case with bank branches, or according to products, such as Ford's separate divisions for separate vehicle types.

● The holding company is a group of independent companies controlled by a co-ordinating group, which commonly consists of the CEOs of each company.

● The project team is a technical group within a larger business structure created to achieve a particular goal or carry out a particular task.

● The matrix system first became popular during the 1970s. It consists of a complex combination of structures that includes divisional and functional business structures and project teams. The matrix system was first developed by the U.S. National Aeronatutics and Space Association (NASA).

● The networking structure has arisen as a result of the advances in technology and communications systems of recent years. Especially important has been the proliferation of personal computers and widespread access to the Internet. This has meant that more people than ever before can now work from home and can still communicate with colleagues, transfer work, and be managed effectively.

Middle management

In each of the above structures it may be seen that beneath the senior managers there are further groupings (departments and divisions)

ABOVE: Deutsche Bank chairman Rolf Breuer addresses shareholders at the bank's annual general meeting in Frankfurt-am-Main, Germany, in 1999.

LEFT: Shareholders appoint a board of executive directors to run their firms. Staff reports to managers, and managers are responsible to the board.

that are connected to the top by a bureaucratic chain of command. At the heads of these groupings are a further level of managers more specialized than the senior management. They are the middle managers, whose job is to link the top level and the first level of management. They coordinate and carry out the policies of top management.

In carrying out the company's established policies, the middle managers often use another level of management, namely, supervisors. Supervisors—otherwise known as team leaders—are responsible for ensuring that the work is done. They oversee the scheduling of work, the maintenance of equipment, and the work routines. Typically, supervisors have greater specialized, technical expertise than those above them and below them. This tripartite division of management is known as the management pyramid. Below the management hierarchy in the organizational pyramid are nonmanagement employees, comprising both administrative and production staff.

When ownership and control are not divided, as they are not under sole proprietors, partnerships, and small limited liability companies, the owners act as managers/entrepreneurs, and they are therefore self-employed. With the division of ownership and control—as with large corporations—the managers and other staff are all employees of the company: they do not own the business, but they are paid by it.

Some employees have permanent employment—that is, long-term work rewarded by a monthly salary. Other employees have temporary employment or short-term work rewarded by weekly or daily wages. Employees who work more than 16 hours per week are full time; those who work less are part time. In general, full-time, permanent employees enjoy the most rights and are the most organized.

Employers require employees to work in accordance with the terms of their contracts. Contracts usually demand that employees arrive on time and work the full number of hours

Key personnel in a modern firm

- Shareholder: owns a stake or share in the company. Votes on membership of board of directors and receives dividends from the company's profits.
- Chief executive officer (CEO): most senior position in the business, overseeing internal operations and external opportunities. Needs to be experienced, successful and have considerable expertise. Must be decisive, communicative, and confident. Plays a major role in the culture, structure, and direction of the business.
- Presidents, vice-presidents: report to CEO and are usually responsible for successful operation of specialized areas of the

business. Must have technical expertise and skill in specific areas such as marketing, finance, production, research and development, and personnel.
- Managers: can come from junior, middle, or senior ranks. Must ensure area of responsibility that is delegated to him or her is run efficiently and successfully. Takes care of the day-to-day running of a defined function.
- Supervisors: first managerial level, responsible for a specific team. Ensures the tasks are accomplished.
- Operators: frontline staff or workforce. The people who actually carry out the tasks that have been delegated to them.

Key departments in a modern firm

- Human resources (HR) or personnel: tasks include defining jobs and requirements, recruitment, contracts of employment, disciplinary procedures, staff training, and administering pensions. Department should also ensure employment corresponds to legal requirements, especially in areas of equal opportunities and health and safety.
- Operations or production: the organization of systems, personnel, and machinery needed to create goods or services. It involves plant layout, maintaining machinery, purchasing, scheduling, quality control, and transportation.
- Finance: specialized area involving accountancy and book keeping, the provision of financial statements for internal and external consumption, and budgeting. The work of the department is vital to the future plans of the business by reporting accurately and swiftly on the current situation. It is also vital in complying with legal requirements of business.
- Sales and marketing: important role in planning, pricing, distribution, and promotion of the goods/services. The promotional strategy includes advertising, personal selling, sales promotion, and publicity. Also has public relations (PR) function in creating a positive image of the company.
- Research and development (R&D): highly specialized department that plays an important role in technological industries. Responsible for the development of new products or the improvement of old ones, thus playing an important role in the future direction of the firm.

agreed with their employer to the best of their ability. Among the employer's other expectations are reasonable and responsible behavior, obedience to line managers, conscientious work carried out in good faith, trustworthiness, and honesty. In return, each employee has the right to the regular and correct payment of agreed and legal wages, safe working conditions that comply with health and safety legislation, and some security of contract.

Labor unions

Employees often combine into unions, which may be organized by industry, sector, or trade. The largest labor union in the United States is the Teamsters Union (established in 1903), representing truck drivers, and workers in related industries, such as aviation. Unions may sometimes entertain a broader agenda, but their primary function is to advise employees on their rights, protect those rights, and advance the interests of employees' by negotiating with management on their behalf.

Typically, unions will seek increases in wages and salaries, reductions in working hours, and improvements in working conditions. The process of negotiating these conditions is known as "collective bargaining." Another important task of unions is to protect members from the infringement of their rights—most commonly in breaches of contract or cases of unfair dismissal. The union principle has always been that a group of workers acting in harmony will get a fairer hearing and a better deal than any one individual will be able to negotiate on his or her own.

During times of conflict with employers unions may use such weapons as work-to-rule, strikes, or boycotts to persuade employers to change their course of action on an issue. With this in mind and to advance cooperation and increase business efficiency, many firms recognize trade unions and actively involve them in the processes of wage and contract negotiation. Many governments also provide arbitration and judicial machinery for the resolution of otherwise insoluble conflicts. As such, unions, alongside the different strata of employees, divisions, and the departments, play an important part in the running of the modern business.

BELOW LEFT: It is the responsibility of production supervisors to ensure the efficiency of equipment and staff. They are expected to draw any problems to the attention of the firm's managers.

How a business works

The fundamental objective of nearly all business enterprises is to make a profit for their owners or shareholders. Here we take a closer look at some of the strategies most commonly used in pursuit of this end.

We are all familiar with business units. We recognize them when we see them, and we have direct or indirect dealings with them every day of our lives. Each time we buy something from the local store or supermarket, for example, we deal directly with the retailer involved and indirectly with all of the other firms whose activities have combined to produce the goods we buy. Whenever we turn on a light or switch on the TV, we deal with firms.

How businesses make decisions

In the previous chapter we looked at the history behind business organizations, the kind of firms, management structures, and people one might expect to find in the modern business world (*see* page 6, An introduction to business). We now turn to how these firms and businesses make their decisions. These decisions are mainly about what to produce, where to produce it, how much to make or provide of a good or service, and the price that should be charged for this good or service. Producers do not necessarily use pure economic theory when they make these decisions—they may not look at the production function they face, for example, nor at the shape of their marginal cost and marginal revenue curves (*see* Figure 4, page 43). Nevertheless theory can be used to predict and explain most decisions that businesses make, and the way that they behave under different market conditions. Therefore in order to see how a business works, it is important first to understand the economic theory that lies behind the decision-making that drives modern-day firms and corporations.

Firms and markets

Firms are basically units of ownership and control. They own equipment and often the premises on which production is carried out. They also own some or all of the raw materials and control the uses to which these commodities are put. Firms can take a variety of forms. The local store and gas station are both production units, as are the world's greatest multinationals such as Ford, General

LEFT: The term business is used to describe commercial enterprises of all sizes, from the largest multinational to the smallest deli.

BELOW: When you buy a newspaper, you are involving yourself in a range of businesses—the newsstand, the paper itself, and—indirectly—the businesses that advertise in it.

Corporate governance

Corporate governance refers to the way in which corporations are run for the benefit of their shareholders, management, employees, customers, suppliers, distributors, and so on. Large corporations in the United States are joint stock companies, and Figure 1 illustrates the nature of such organizations.

The owners of the corporation are its shareholders, and at the annual general meeting they appoint a board of directors and auditors to act on their behalf. The board of directors is responsible for controling the company and, if necessary, for appointing managers to act on their behalf. Corporate governance is therefore important to shareholders because they invest funds in the corporation but appoint managers to run it.

This separation of ownership from control provides an example of the principal-agent problem, in which a dilemma exists when both groups have different aims. In the case of corporations it might be argued that agents (executives and managers) are expected to pursue their own interests (salaries and income) at the expense of principals (the shareholders), who might wish to achieve higher profits. It is certainly true that principals tend to be less well-informed about company performance than their agents, which is why they appoint agents in the first place.

So how are the activities of agents to be controled? In the United States, and in other countries such as the United Kingdom, there is a market-based system of corporate governance. Poor company performance, reflected in lower-than-expected returns to shareholders, will encourage the sale of shares. Inevitably, share prices in poorly performing corporations will fall. This signals shareholder dissatisfaction to the board of directors and may lead, if performance does not improve, to a takeover, when one corporation buys 51 percent of the voting share capital in another corporation. When this happens, many senior managers in the corporation taken over are almost certain to lose their jobs. It is argued that this provides an incentive to ensure that companies perform well.

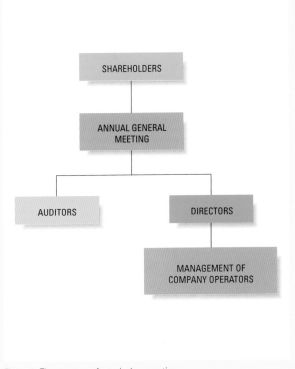

Figure 1 The structure of a typical corporation.

Motors, and Chrysler, which have their operations spread over several countries in order to maximize their market reach and minimize their costs.

All firms operate in at least one market. Many people think of a market as a place where buyers and sellers meet to transact business, as they do, for example, at an automobile auction. Yet in the real world the term "market" embraces much more than this. It is not strictly necessary for buyers and sellers of products to meet at all. In economic theory a market is really any arrangement or set of arrangements that bring buyers of different goods and services into contact with sellers of those goods and services.

According to this definition, an automobile auction is a market. So is the local supermarket. So too are the Commodity Markets in New York, Chicago, and Philadelphia and the New York Stock Exchange. Among numerous less obvious examples of markets are local newspapers, which are part of the property market because they advertise houses and business premises for sale and thus bring

LEFT: Stop-and-go gas stations such as this one in Houston, Texas, are the retail outlets of vast multinational oil producers.

buyers and sellers of the same capital good into contact with each other. As well as disseminating information, the Internet is a market because it brings together sellers and potential buyers of almost every imaginable product worldwide.

Profit—the basic aim

All firms exist to achieve a particular goal or goals. While different firms might have different goals, all private-sector firms—that is, firms other than those run by the national government—must make a profit on their operations: in other words, their revenue must be greater than their costs. The simplest definition of profit is the amount that is left over after all accounting costs have been met. Accounting costs are the dollar costs of production a firm incurs when it buys its raw materials, hires labor, and so on. Sales revenue is the income the firm receives from selling its product or products. Thus, in the simplest definition:

Profit = Sales Revenue - Accounting Cost.

For firms to stay in business, profit must be positive in most years, but in certain cases firms might temporarily accept a negative profit—that is, a loss. For the moment, however, we will concentrate on the level of profit firms might aim to achieve.

The assumption that most people traditionally make about nearly all firms apart from charities is that they aim to earn as much money as they can as quickly and as cheaply as they possibly can—that is, their goal is profit maximization. Firms are held to have maximized their profit when the difference between their sales revenues and their accounting costs is as great as it can be. There are several good reasons for assuming that firms aim to maximize profit. After all, it is surely better to have greater profit than less profit. And yet, despite the appealing logic and simplicity of this argument, in the real world we find that firms do not always regard profit maximization as their main aim: they may, for example, choose instead to maximize sales revenue or go at full tilt for a larger share of the market.

LEFT: A meeting of shareholders—people who invest in a firm in order to share in any profits it may make on trading.

Sales revenue maximization

Instead of profit maximization, in certain circumstances some firms might accept a lower level of profit and aim instead at sales revenue maximization. Whether this situation arises depends to some extent on the nature of the firm. Sole proprietors are more likely to aim at profit maximization than large corporations because the sole proprietor's profit is his or her income. Large corporations, by contrast, are run by salaried managers rather than by their owners (shareholders), and there is considerable evidence to show that executives' salaries are often linked to revenue—that is, total income before costs have been deducted—rather than to profit—net income after all costs have been deducted. For obvious reasons this will influence the way the managers run the business. Management executives might also aim to maximize sales rather than profit because revenue may be used to finance new projects, whereas profit will be distributed to shareholders.

Maximizing market share

Another possibility is that firms might aim to maximize their share of the market. The rationale for this is that larger firms have more security than smaller firms. Every year tens of thousands of small firms go bust, but larger corporations generally manage to weather the roughest economic storms. In addition, larger firms often have lower production costs than smaller firms simply because larger firms can negotiate a favorable price at which to buy raw materials in bulk. But probably the most important reason why firms may seek to maximize their market share is that senior managers' salaries are often linked to the size of the firm rather than to its profit. Although this approach may appear self-serving—as indeed it might be in the most extreme cases—it may be justifiable if there are thought to be long-term benefits from growing in order to achieve the greatest possible economies of scale. Firms that have grown to this level are sometimes said to have achieved critical mass.

Why firms do not always close down when they make a loss

When firms make a loss, they might sometimes be prepared to write it off —that is, cancel the entry in the account books— if they believe that it is only a temporary reverse. At other times, it is in their interests to close down immediately. Why is this?

In the short run the firm must meet its fixed costs of production—such as mortgage repayments and insurance charges—even if it produces nothing. This implies that for as long as the firm can earn sufficient revenue to cover its total variable costs, it will be no worse off if it undertakes production in the short run than if it produces nothing. It follows from this that if total revenue exceeds total variable cost, the firm will

make a smaller loss if it undertakes production in the short run; and where total revenue is less than total variable cost, the firm will make a smaller loss if it withdraws from the industry and produces nothing.

It is important to note that while a firm can bear a maximum loss equal to its fixed costs in the short run, it cannot do so in the long run. If the price of its output does not rise, or its costs fall so that the firm earns a profit in the long run, it will be forced to leave the industry.

For this loss situation the same rules apply to all private-sector firms regardless of size.

Nonmaximizing goals

Another approach to firm behavior stresses the importance of group dynamics. This simply means that firms are made up of different groups: managers, shareholders, workers, and so on. Each group sets its own goal, and the goal adopted by the firm depends on which of these groups has the greatest influence. This approach to firm behavior implies that goals change when a different group begins to dominate one or more of the others. Firms are thus sometimes said to be "accountancy-led" or "marketing-led."

Satisficing

Behaviorist analyses of firms are based on the belief that in practise, managers cannot be sure when they are maximizing profit, sales, or market share. They know what the levels of profit, sales, and market share are, but they do not know for sure whether they are at their maximum potential levels. Instead of a maximizing approach, they therefore settle for minimum acceptable levels of achievement. Firms that adopt this approach are said to satisfice rather than maximize. This does not necessarily imply that satisficing results in a lower level of achievement, because as each level of achievement is reached, performance targets could be revised upward. Figure 2 (*below*) illustrates this process.

If firms adopt a satisficing approach, there is no way of knowing which goal will emerge as the most desirable. Different groups in an organization might have different objectives that may sometimes conflict with each other. For example, workers might want higher wages; and if shareholders want higher prof-

its, a conflict of interests will then arise. This conflict can be resolved only when one group achieves ascendancy over and dictates terms to the others.

Production

Whatever the goal of a firm, it must always produce an output—that is, finished goods or services—in order to attain it. Production is defined as the transformation of inputs—natural resources, raw materials, labor, machinery, and so on—into an output. The term output might also be used to describe the quantity of output produced in a given period.

ABOVE: In layman's terms this is lumber, but economists call it land because it is one of the earth's natural resources.

BELOW: Mining is a major source of economic wealth. The products unearthed by this process come from the earth and are therefore also a form of the resource classified as land.

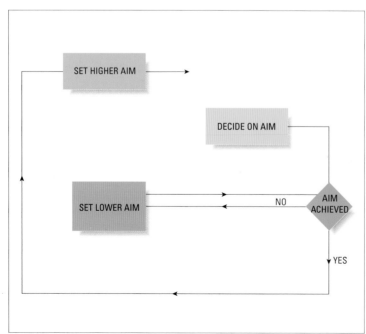

Figure 2 *Setting goals that are based on satisficing.*

SET HIGHER AIM

DECIDE ON AIM

SET LOWER AIM

NO

AIM ACHIEVED

YES

Thus an automobile firm might have a production target of two million vehicles a year. Productivity, on the other hand, is a measure of the efficiency with which output is achieved. For example, say that 10 workers initially produce 100 units of output per hour. If this level of output later rises to 110 units per hour, for whatever reason, in economic terms productivity is said to have increased by 10 percent.

Resources used in production

Every form of business production requires the input of one or more resources. Economists usually identify four different categories of resource, namely, land, labor, capital, and entrepreneurship.

Land is defined as all the natural resources that can be used in production. The term therefore refers to the earth's surface as well as to the minerals and ores it contains, the sea and its contents, and so on. By this definition fish, for example, count as land.

Labor refers to human input, both mental and physical. Most people's income depends on their ability to sell their labor, and by and large, differences in earnings reflect the different skills possessed by workers. In economics the skills possessed by a nation's labor force are said to be part of that country's capital stock. Education and training, through which the labor force acquires its skills, are therefore referred to as investments in human capital. Investment in human capital is important because the more highly skilled a nation's labor force, the more productive it is. From this it frequently—but not necessarily—follows that the nation as a whole will become more prosperous.

Capital is defined as any asset created to assist the production process. Two types of capital are often identified in business: circulating capital and fixed capital. Circulating capital (*see* Figure 3, above) is capital that is used up in the course of production because its form changes during production. It includes assets such as raw materials, semifinished products, and inventories.

The fixed assets of a business include premises, machinery, and tools. These capital assets undergo no transformation during the production process and retain their original form throughout.

Of all resources entrepreneurship is probably the easiest to recognize but the most difficult to define. Broadly, an entrepreneur may be described as an economic agent who perceives market opportunities and assembles the factors of production to exploit them in a firm. Economists agree that an entrepreneur is a risk-taker because his or her income depends on the success of the business. If a business makes a profit, the entrepreneur's

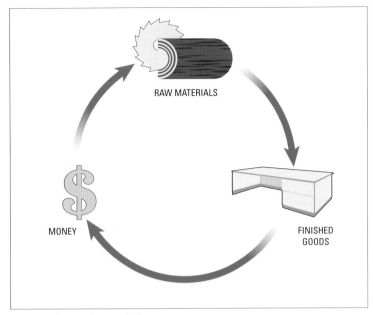

Figure 3 Circulating capital.

reward is positive. Conversely, if the business makes a loss, the entrepreneur will have to bear that loss. The entrepreneur's role is therefore to identify schemes with profit-making potential and put them into practice: there is no doubt that without the entrepreneur, production would be extremely limited.

BELOW: A washing machine factory in Naples, Italy. Goods like this are assembled in large centers of population, cities to and from which there are well-developed and cheap means of transportation.

Location of industry

When any firm starts up in business, it is important for its owners or managers to decide where it is going to buy or rent its premises. Many factors may influence this choice of location—for example, sometimes key personnel prefer to live in a particular part of the country. However, successful factories and business premises are seldom sited solely on whim—economic considerations are, of course, of paramount importance.

Transportation costs

In order to maximize their profit, industries endeavor to keep their costs as low as possible. Thus manufacturers of consumer durables, such as washing machines, refrigerators, and automobiles—which are all heavy and bulky in relation to their value—tend to locate themselves in large cities in order to minimize the cost of transporting the heavy equipment that is their stock in trade. This is because it is generally cheaper to transport goods to and from large population centers along established lines of communication than to and from remote country locations.

Some heavy industries—such as coal mining and steel manufacture—locate themselves as close as possible to the point at which their raw materials are extracted from the ground. This is because the cost of transporting them to another location would be so great that it would eat up any possible overall profit. A diamond, by contrast—which weighs very little but may be worth a fortune—can be transported at low cost and with little effort to almost any part of the world.

A firm's location may also be determined by the need to be close to—or at least within easy reach of—its market. One firm may set up in an out-of-town shopping mall confident that customers will drive out to it along highways. Other businesses, such as newsstands and hairdressers, may have to rent premises much closer to the people they hope to attract.

Despite these considerations, the importance of transportation declined significantly in the latter part of the 20th century. That is because major improvements have taken place in transportation facilities: in the means of carriage (trucks, ships, and airplanes); in the techniques of handling, particularly of bulk goods (forklifts, containers); and in the transportation network itself (a proliferation of freeways and cargo terminals). There have also been significant changes in the industrial landscape, with heavy goods becoming relatively less important, and newer industries—computing, for example—producing goods for which the transportation costs are much less significant.

Cost and availability of labor

The availability of labor and its cost can also be major influences on an industry's choice of location. In the United States labor costs are cheaper in the south than in the north, but globally labor costs are cheaper in the countries of the developing world. Many U.S. firms now locate new plants abroad rather than in home states. There might be many reasons for this, but cheaper labor is one of the most important considerations.

Acquired advantages

For whatever historical reason firms are located where they are, over time they often acquire additional advantages that help keep them there and attract new firms to the same locations. These acquired advantages are usu

BELOW: In the second half of the 20th century the increased capacity of container ships greatly improved the international transportation of goods.

Ben and Jerry's business plan

Not everyone sets out a formal business plan covering all of the points mentioned in the text. The successful partnership of Ben Cohen and Jerry Greenfield, for example, takes a highly unconventional approach to business. The two men decided to start their own ice cream firm after taking a $5 correspondence course from Pennsylvania State University.

When Ben and Jerry started making ice cream, they had little financial backing, and their only asset was an old car. Undeterred, they borrowed $12,000 mainly from friends and family, and started up in a converted gas station in Burlington, Vermont. Their aim was simply to make the best ice cream they could. At first they relied on walk-in business, but they soon began supplying local stores and restaurants. They now have establishments in many places all over the world, including Moscow, Russia.

Typical of Ben and Jerry's idiosyncratic approach is their belief that a business should give something back to the community. To this end they donate 7.5 percent of their pretax profit to nonprofit organizations and individuals working for social improvement. Their wage structure is equally unusual—they operate a five-to-one policy in which the salary of the highest paid employee can never be more than five times greater than that of the lowest paid employee.

Ben and Jerry have been extremely successful, but they are gifted mavericks, and their unconventional approach to business is not recommended as a model. Comprehensive business planning is more likely to lead to success for most people.

RIGHT: Ice cream manufacturers Ben Cohen and Jerry Greenfield enjoying their product. The Ben and Jerry business formula has brought these two men great success but is unlikely to work for others.

ally referred to as external economies of scale, and they arise for several reasons. One important external economy is the development locally of ancillary industries—firms that exist wholly or mainly to service and supply the main industry. Wherever a manufacturing industry is located, in the same vicinity there will also be firms that supply specialized machinery, components, packaging, and so on. In the same area preexisting or specially built local colleges will provide courses in the skills relevant to the main industry. The effect of these external economies is to ensure that existing locations confer cost advantages on new and expanding firms.

Making a business plan

Before starting up, every firm should prepare a detailed business plan, the contents of which are of vital importance to the future development of the enterprise. The business plan should give a detailed account of what to produce, how to transform inputs into outputs, and how to make profits. The fol-

lowing are some of the questions that a business plan should address in detail.

Every business has to produce something, and this is probably the earliest decision that has to be made by owners who are planning to set up a new firm. There must be a working role for the owner or owners and (where there is a difference) the manager or man-

BELOW: The Ford assembly plant in Chicago, Illinois. The development of mass production techniques brought more and more goods within the financial reach of more people than ever before.

agers. This may seem obvious, and yet many businesses fail not because they have no possible future but because of misunderstandings about the precise role and responsibilities of their owners. In deciding the parts to be played by the different parties in the firm, decisions must also be made about the way in which production is to be organized. What techniques are to be used, for example, and in what proportions will the firm combine the resources that are used to make the product?

A business plan must also clearly define the intended market for the firm's produce. It is not sufficient simply to found a company on the abstract decision to, for example, produce clothing and then hope that customers will be found after the business is up and running.

Once the target market has been identified, the business plan must then give a detailed account of the means by which the firm will draw itself to the attention of potential consumers. Probably the most difficult task for any business is persuading consumers to purchase its product in preference to other competing brands. Making sure that this happens involves the preparation of a detailed plan for advertising and marketing and a bud-

get for both. Distribution networks—mail order, local supermarkets, trucking firms, etc.—must also be identified, as must a practical method of reaching them.

The business plan should also include a description of how the firm is to be financed and the cost of borrowing the money. The level of finance that will be required depends to some extent on the projected levels of output. Finally, a good business plan will be needed to convince banks and other potential lenders to advance the money needed to start the firm. If the plan is not well thought out and clearly presented, it is unlikely to attract the necessary investment.

Division of labor

Most firms or businesses—even those with only two or three employees—can benefit from specialization or the division of labor. It is important for a firm to decide to what extent it can benefit from specialization, and how best to take advantage of this concept. The division of labor involves breaking down the production process into a number of specialized tasks. Even the most cursory glance around a modern factory will provide examples of division of labor. However, divi-

LEFT: At some time in their lives many people become economic migrants—they move to a new area in order to take up a better-paid job.

The mobility of Americans

Every year about 10 percent of American workers change jobs. Most of them are younger workers, and this is hardly surprising because younger people classically make frequent changes as they search for a job they enjoy, and which offers them suitable long-term prospects. The cost of switching jobs is relatively low among the young—they have not acquired experience and marketable skills; and so when they leave a job, they leave little in the way of skills behind them. This makes it easy for them to change career direction and easy for their current employers to let them go.

Older workers, by contrast, have both invested and had invested in them more time and money as they have acquired experience and skills. Quitting one job for another involves leaving behind a certain amount of expertise. Thus they might have to start another job on a lower rung of the promotional ladder. Yet, despite these disadvantages, about eight percent of the U.S. workforce aged between mid-30s and mid-40s still change jobs every year. Only those fairly close to retirement have

low mobility. Retraining probably isn't worth the time, effort, and expense for these people, and there are relatively few opportunities for them anyway.

In the geographical sense Americans are highly mobile. On average, about eight percent of the U.S. population aged five and over move at least once a year. The amount of mobility varies between regions, and in recent decades there has been considerable movement of workers from the Rustbelt to the Sunbelt. This is largely explained by the decline of heavy industries (automobiles, steel, and coal) in the Northeast and Midwest and the enormous expansion of the service and light manufacturing sectors (especially personal computers) in the South and West.

A high degree of workforce mobility is relatively easy to achieve over time. As young people leave high school and college, the opportunities available at that time will limit their career choices. Declining industries will be cutting back on recruitment, whereas expanding industries will have a greater number of career opportunities.

sion of labor is not simply confined to manufacturing. If you visit an attorney's office, for example, you will find lawyers specializing in different branches of the law.

Division of labor is particularly common in manufacturing industries because it makes possible tremendous increases in efficiency. When automobiles were hand-built individually by highly skilled craftsmen, they were available only to a very small number of wealthy people. It was Henry Ford's use of division-of-labor techniques on the "Model T" production lines in Detroit, Michigan, that first brought automobiles within the budget of many ordinary Americans. From this we can see that division of labor is associated both with standardization and with lower costs. Henry Ford's much quoted dictum "You can have any color you like as long as it's black" attests the extent to which standardization was achieved on his early production line—range of choice was sacrificed in order to achieve greater accessibility.

Lower cost, greater choice

It has sometimes been suggested that standardization removes individuality of expression, but this seldom bears close examination. For example, look around your school or college. How often do you see your friends wearing exactly the same item of clothing as yourself or eating the same brand of ice cream? Probably not very often, if ever. Similarly, when you go shopping, how often do you look for something different and yet fail to find it? Very infrequently. Next time you notice the range of choice that is now widely available to vast numbers of people, think for

a moment about the old Model T Ford. Before standardization very few people owned automobiles. By reducing the price of many goods to affordable levels, standardization has in fact increased the range of goods available to most of us.

But why are goods cheaper when they are produced in this standardized way? Because standardization enables firms to make savings through both the bulk purchase of raw materials and more efficient use of their machinery. These serve to lower the unit cost of production.

Mobility of labor

Mobility refers to the ease with which a significant part of the production process—such as labor or capital—can switch between tasks, geographical location, or occupation. Mobility of labor is an important consideration for any firm hoping to employ workers with a particular skill, for example, since it may have to recruit from beyond its immediate geographical surroundings.

Differences in compensation (wages and fringe benefits) are among the most important factors that influence the degree of mobility among American workers. Semiskilled workers living in Providence, Rhode Island, for example, are unlikely to move to Chicago, Illinois, for only a slight raise in wages. Similarly, car mechanics are unlikely to quit their jobs and retrain if they have no prospect of an acceptable increase in compensation.

A mobile labor force is important if a business—and the country in general—is to respond to changes in demand for its products, such as may be caused by exchange rate depreciation or improvements in technology.

While a high degree of mobility is considered desirable for businesses, too much mobility can be bad. When workers move from one region to another, pressure on social capital (schools, hospitals, and roads) falls, while pressure on social capital rises in the area to which they have moved. For the economy as a whole it could be argued that this is a waste of resources, since there will be underutilization of social capital in some areas and increased pressure in other areas.

Also, it is younger workers who tend to move most readily, and so declining areas tend to have aging populations. This makes these locations less and less attractive for new firms and might increase their chances of becoming economically depressed—an economically depressed area is characterized by relatively high rates of unemployment and relatively low levels of income per head.

By contrast, an excessive degree of labor mobility might not be good for the economy of the country as a whole. Firms invest a great deal of time and large sums of money in training their workforce. As with any investment, they aim to increase their returns as a result. Yet a high degree of labor turnover, as workers seek new and better-paid opportunities elsewhere, might discourage firms from investing in human capital and thus result in a skill shortage.

Changes in inputs and productivity

If a firm is successful, it will soon have to address the problems caused by an increase in the number of people who want to buy the particular good or service it is producing. The management will then need to decide how best to respond to this rising demand.

When demand for a product is rising, the firms that produce it will almost certainly raise their levels of production—that is, they will make more of whatever it is they sell. To achieve this end, they will hire more resources (workers and equipment). Often in

BELOW: In the United States the decline in Rustbelt industries such as steelmaking has been balanced by the growth of Sunbelt businesses such as computer manufacture.

ABOVE: *Trouser pressing at a textile factory. More people specializing in a few parts of the production process is often more profitable than having one person perform the whole process.*

these circumstances their output will increase relatively quickly, perhaps within as little as a month or even a week. However, if firms are already operating at full capacity, such rapid changes in output are unlikely to be possible. In order to expand, firms will require additional factory space or other fixed assets, and they might take months to construct or install. Economists refer to these two different response periods as, respectively, the short run and the long run.

Economists distinguish the short run from the long run not simply as fixed periods, but rather as the times required to change the input of different resources. Some factors of production are referred to as variable factors, and others are referred to as fixed factors. Variable factors, as the name suggests, are those whose input can be changed quickly and easily. Unskilled labor, raw materials, and power to drive machinery are all examples of the variable factors of production. Fixed factors, by contrast, are more durable and long-lasting and take longer to acquire or install. Skilled labor, factory premises, and so on are examples of fixed factors.

In the short run firms may be able to increase production by altering the input of variable factors and working existing fixed factors more intensely. If the demand for a firm's product increases, one possible response is to increase overtime working. If this course of action is taken, the firm will use more power and raw materials, but the extent to which output can be increased will still be limited by, for example, the number of machines the firm owns or the limited available space in which new machines can be installed. In the long run, however, it is generally possible to alter the input of all the factors of production.

It is impossible to quantify the short run and the long run within any fixed period because the time required to change factor inputs will vary from industry to industry. In some industries, particularly those relying heavily on the input of unskilled labor, the long run might be no more than a few months. However, in other industries, such as steelmaking or oil refining, the short run may well extend for several years because that is the length of time it takes to plan new plants, get approval, construct them, and bring them into operation.

Average and marginal products

A firm that wants to expand its output must make decisions about which inputs it needs to increase—whether to increase the amount of raw materials, or employ more workers and, if so, how many, whether to buy another machine, build another factory, and so on.

A study of production reveals the relationship between input and output. The production function tells us that quantity produced depends on the input of capital and the input of labor. However, the production function does not tell the full story because when firms change their inputs in the short run, output is unlikely to change in direct proportion—if the

The law of diminishing marginal returns

The law of diminishing marginal returns is usually illustrated with a simple example such as that shown in the table below:

Number of workers	Total Product	Average Product	Marginal Product
1	5.0	5.0	5.0
2	11.0	5.5	6.0
3	21.0	7.0	10.0
4	36.0	9.0	15.0
5	50.0	10.0	14.0
6	54.0	9.0	4.0

Up to the employment of the fourth worker the firm experiences increasing marginal returns as employment rises. In other words, marginal product—the additional total product when one more worker is employed—is rising. Note that although the firm experiences diminishing marginal returns after the employment of the fourth worker, productivity (average product) goes on rising until after the employment of the fifth worker. The operation of the law of diminishing marginal returns is universal—every firm, regardless of size, is bound by its rules.

firm employs twice as many workers or twice as many machines, for example, it will not necessarily produce twice as much output.

To analyze the effect of changes in inputs, especially labor, on output, economists distinguish between average product and marginal product. Average product is simply the total output divided by the number of workers employed—in other words, the amount produced per worker. Marginal product is a more difficult concept. It is the increase in total output that occurs when one more worker (the marginal worker) is employed. A simple example to illustrate these concepts is given in the box above.

The table here shows that as the number of workers employed increases from one to four, the total product becomes progressively larger. Over this range of employment marginal product is increasing—each worker adds more to production than the previous worker—and thus we may say that the firm experiences increasing marginal returns. However, as employment rises beyond four workers, total product starts to rise at a diminishing rate—that is, each successive worker adds less to the total product than the previous additional worker. Marginal product is now falling, and thus we say that, after the employment of the fifth worker, the firm begins to experience diminishing marginal returns.

Disparities in the marginal productivity of labor are not caused by differences in the quality of the workforce employed. Instead, they are caused by the changing proportions of fixed factors (such as machines) and variable factors (such as raw materials) in the production function. At low levels of output fixed factors are underutilized. As employment rises,

it becomes possible for workers to specialize, and so marginal product rises. However, this favorable arrangement cannot continue indefinitely. At higher levels of output the ratio of fixed to variable factors becomes less favorable, and marginal product falls in conse-

BELOW: Chefs are a good example of a variable cost—more of them will be needed to increase the number of people a restaurant can serve.

quence. This may happen, for example, when a fifth worker starts to get in the way of the other four taken on earlier. When something like this happens, we begin to see in operation the law of diminishing marginal returns.

Economies of scale

We have already seen what happens to firms when they are faced with changes of output in the short run. Now we turn our attention to what may happen when firms change the input of all factors of production, something they can do in the long run.

In simple terms, if a firm receives greater input—more machinery, more capital, more raw materials, more laborers—than before, its production will increase by a ratio of more than one. It may be, for example, that if twice as many people are taken on to operate twice as many machines, the firm will produce more than twice as many products as it did before. Increased productivity of this type is said to be an economy of scale. Economies of scale are often referred to as the advantages of size,

and they are important because they are associated with falling average costs of production per unit of a good or service. This is why the products of larger firms are often considerably cheaper than similar goods produced by smaller firms.

Economies of scale arise for many reasons. Larger firms can acquire funds at lower rates than smaller firms because they present less of a risk to lenders. The average cost of inputs is also less for larger firms than for smaller firms because they are able to buy in bulk. The average cost of shipping a ton of crude oil across the ocean, for example, is many times cheaper if we use a supertanker than if we use several smaller tankers because costs do not rise proportionately.

Diseconomies of scale

However, economies of scale cannot increase indefinitely—they cease to be achievable once they reach a point of constant returns. Alternatively, there may come a point at which output starts to increase less than

BELOW: Checking jars for flaws in a food-processing plant. Quality control is an important part of the production process of any consumer good and an unavoidable cost to any business of this type.

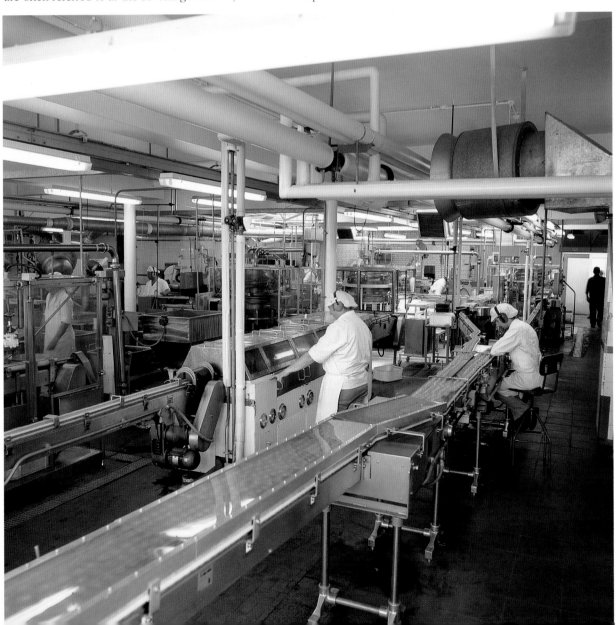

proportionately with any change of inputs (that is, by a factor of less than one). Average production costs may begin to rise. When increasing size leads to higher costs per unit, the firm is said to be experiencing diseconomies of scale (*see* How firms behave in the real world, page 80).

Costs of production

Costs of production form an important part of the decisions firms make on how much to produce and what prices to charge. If a firm produces more than it can sell at a particular price, for example, its costs will be greater than the money it is receiving, and the firm will consequently make a loss. If it continues to make a loss, the firm will eventually go out of business.

Economists study the types of costs that firms face, the ways in which these costs vary as output increases, and the factors that affect changes in firms' costs and revenues. They do this in order to understand how firms go about setting prices and deciding on the most efficient levels of output to produce.

It is usual to begin any analysis of a firm's production costs by identifying and distinguishing between its fixed costs and its variable costs. We saw earlier that a firm's inputs can be thought of as fixed or variable: fixed costs are costs incurred on fixed assets—such as buildings—while variable costs are, of course, incurred on variable factors, such as raw materials.

Fixed costs

Fixed costs are easy to identify. The input of fixed factors does not change as output changes, and therefore fixed costs do not change as output changes. However, if you own a business, you will quickly discover another feature of fixed costs, which is that they are incurred even if no output is produced! Fixed costs include such items as rent or mortgage repayments on premises, insurance charges, and depreciation on assets, for example, the fall in the value of machinery over time and as a result of its use.

For most businesses depreciation is the most significant of all fixed costs. One of the most unwelcome aspects of depreciation is that it affects even assets that remain unused.

BELOW: The grading and sorting machines at this egg-processing factory are all fixed assets.

This is because any machine purchased in one financial year is always worth less the following year (*see* Finance and accounting, page 48).

Variable and marginal costs

As their name suggests, variable costs—such as the amounts spent on the purchase of raw materials—vary directly with output. Indeed, they are sometimes referred to as direct costs. Firms incur variable costs only if they undertake production: the greater the level of output produced, the greater the level of variable costs thereby incurred. In this respect they are unlike fixed costs, which are incurred whether there is production or not.

Marginal cost is defined as the change in total cost the business incurs when it produces one more unit of output. It is therefore the increased variable cost the business incurs when output rises by one unit. Variable costs vary directly with output, but they do not vary proportionately because of the effects of increasing and diminishing marginal returns (*see* box, page 40).

The changes in total variable costs brought about by increasing and diminishing marginal returns also imply changes in the average variable costs. The relationship between average and marginal product, and average variable and marginal costs is shown in Figure 4.

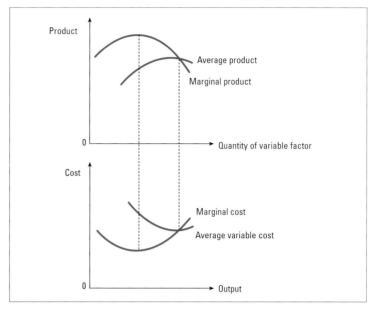

Figure 4 The effect of changes in marginal and average product on marginal and average cost.

BELOW: A jewelry factory in Providence, Rhode Island. All the equipment is a depreciating asset.

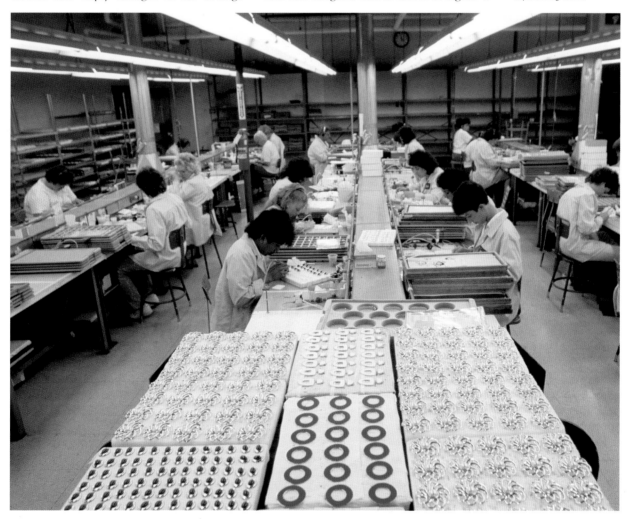

Closing unprofitable mines in the United Kingdom

ABOVE: Throughout the 1980s in the United Kingdom coal mines like this were closed because they were deemed to be unprofitable. Although this made sense for the ruling Conservative Party, there is still controversy about whether it made economic sense.

The British coal industry was nationalized in the 1940s at a time when this fossil fuel was the main producer of the nation's energy. By 1980, however, imported coal had become relatively cheap, an imbalance caused in part by the fact that much foreign coal was government-subsidized, whereas British coal was not. In addition, the ruling Conservative Party under Prime Minister Margaret Thatcher (1979-90) was doctrinally opposed to public ownership. Yet instead of selling off this industry to private firms—as happened with British Aerospace, British Rail, British Steel, the automobile manufacturers Jaguar and Rolls Royce, and several other state-owned firms—the government instructed senior management at the industry's administrative body, the National Coal Board (NCB), to embark on a large-scale closure plan.

In response to this move the traditionally militant National Union of Mineworkers (NUM) instructed its members to withdraw their labor. An acrimonious strike developed, which was often marred by violent clashes between police and demonstrators. The NCB argued that unprofitable mines were uneconomic. However, some economists took—and still take—the view that what has happened in the past is irrelevant to the

present and future conduct of any business. According to them, fixed costs are inescapable, and it is therefore unnecessary to consider them in any decision about pit closures.

This was the NUM's case. They claimed that many of the costs taken into consideration by the NCB when they examined the viability of a mine should not be part of the current assessment. Ill-feeling between the board and the union increased when the former incorporated a wide range of historical items of expenditure into its cost analysis of the current situation. They included the expense of meeting claims for subsidence due to mining operations in the past, pension payments made to former employees who were now retired, and the interest paid on loans that had been used to finance earlier investment. The government and the NCB believed that it would be folly to maintain the mines any longer because doing so would lead to further expenses of the same type—they wanted to avoid sending good money after bad.

U.K. mine closures went ahead, and union resistance was crushed. But the relevance of fixed costs was never fully explored, and many economists felt that the policy could not be justified on economic grounds.

Price discrimination in the airline industry

ABOVE: The world's leading airlines are in a strong position to impose different prices for the same seats on the same flight because in many cases passengers have no real choice about when they fly or which company they fly with.

On any transatlantic flight carrying almost 400 passengers there might be as many as 100 different prices for the same journey. The major reason for such discrepancies is that airlines aim to gain more profit by exploiting differences in the elasticity of demand for passenger travel. Travelers have varying elasticity of demand for a flight partly because of differences in their commitments. Business and professional people, for example, may need to attend a meeting at very short notice, and there might be only one flight they can possibly take. Thus they will have a low elasticity of demand for a particular flight and will be prepared to pay relatively high prices. By contrast, other travelers might have considerable flexibility and might only be prepared to make a reservation after having been offered standby tickets at relatively low prices.

When the firm experiences increasing returns, the marginal product rises, and the marginal cost falls. Conversely, when the firm experiences diminishing returns, marginal product falls, and marginal cost rises.

Average total costs

Average total costs—which are often referred to simply as average costs—can be calculated by dividing the firm's total costs by its total output in units. We know that average fixed costs fall continuously as output expands, and that, initially, the average variable cost falls. It follows that the average total cost curve will also fall to begin with. However, a point will be reached at which the fall in average fixed costs is more than offset by the later increase in average variable costs. This causes an increase in the average total cost of production; the average total cost curve starts to rise.

The firm's revenue

We saw earlier that sales revenue is defined as the income that a firm receives from the sales of its product or products. For each product total revenue is equal to the price at which the product sells multiplied by the quantity sold. Thus we can work out total revenue by means of the simple equation:

$$TR = P \times Q$$

where TR = Total revenue, P = Price of the product, and Q = Quantity of the product sold.

For the purposes of analysis we sometimes write average revenue (AR) instead of price. One reason for this is to avoid the distortions in the figures that may be caused when—as often happens—a manufacturer or wholesaler sells the same product to various clients at different discounts depending on the amount of business they generate. In simple terms it is easy to show that when a firm sells all units of a product at a single price, average revenue and price will be identical.

Marginal revenue

The concept known to economists as marginal revenue is simply the increase in total revenue that is derived from the sale of one more unit. Thus, if a firm sells each unit it produces at $10, marginal revenue is $10. However, unlike marginal cost (which is always positive), marginal revenue might sometimes be negative. The reason for this may be understood if we imagine that a firm sold 1,000 units at $10 each, but to sell one more unit the firm reduced the price of all units to $9.90. What is the change in total revenue as a result of this price reduction? Initially total revenue will be $10 x 1,000 = $10,000, but after the price reduction total revenue = $9.90 x 1,001 = $9,909.90. Thus total revenue falls by $90.1, and so marginal revenue equals -$90.1! You might also wonder why firms would want to sell more units for less revenue. The answer, as we saw above, is that it depends on the firm's aim or objective.

Pricing in practice

No one seriously doubts that a price can exist without a demand for or even a supply of the product in question. Firms control the price they charge for their product, and they determine that price according to some rule. But almost no one who runs a business will say that the price of their product is determined by supply and demand. So what does dictate it?

As we showed above, costs rise as firms increase production according to the law of diminishing returns. However, there are many other reasons why costs might rise. For example, the price of raw materials or the levels of compensation might increase. The supply curve (Figure 5) assumes that all of these other costs are constant. But if for some reason they should rise, they will increase the firm's costs at all levels of output, and the effect will be to shift the supply curve in Figure 6 upward from S_0 to S_1.

Now it is possible to reconcile the "cost-plus" view of price determination—in which an individual firm sets its prices according to costs—with the view that prices are determined by supply and demand in the market as a whole (the market view of price determination). We can reconcile both views by noting that when firms add a markup, the market supply curve shifts so as to ensure equilibrium between supply and demand. The market price thus determined coincides with the firm's notion of cost-plus pricing. So, for example, in Figure 5 S_0 is the supply curve that exists when the firm covers all its pro-

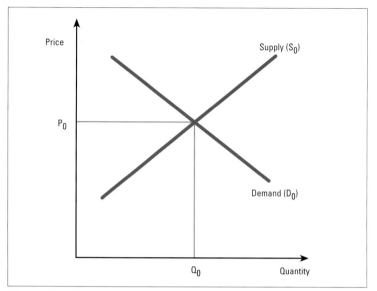

Figure 5 Equilibrium price and quantity.

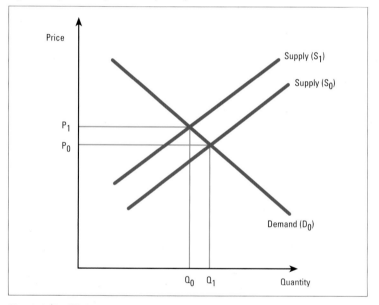

Figure 6 Equilibrium price and quantity with and without firms adding a markup—the "plus" element of cost-plus pricing.

duction costs but makes no profit. Now imagine that the firm adds a markup of $10.00 per unit. Costs will rise by $10.00 at all levels of output, and the supply curve will shift upward, for example, to S_1 (Figure 6, above). Price now rises to P_1. In a free market price is ultimately determined by supply and demand, yet firms set the price of their goods on a cost-plus basis. The market-clearing price and the price at which the firm maximizes its profit are one and the same.

Elasticity

It is important for a firm or business to have some idea of how responsive the demand for its product is to changes in price. If the firm

SEE ALSO:

• Volume 5, page 21: Costs
• Volume 5, page 62: Marginal analysis
• Volume 5, page 82: Price and price theory
• Volume 5, page 86: Production
• Volume 5, page 88: Profit and profit maximization
• Volume 5, page 95: Resources, economic

produces a breakfast cereal, for example, and knows that when it puts the price up, many of its customers will switch to a similar cereal produced by a rival, then it is unlikely to increase the price. It is also important for the firm to know how responsive the quantity supplied can be to changes in price—if the market price for breakfast cereals goes up, how quickly can the firm increase its output to take advantage of the new price?

Calculating PED

The concept known as price elasticity of demand (PED) measures the responsiveness of the quantity of a good or service demanded to a change in the product's price. Similarly, elasticity of supply measures the responsiveness of the quantity supplied to changes in the price of the product. In both cases elasticity is measured by substituting in the following formula:

$$PED = \frac{(\text{Percentage change in quantity})}{(\text{Percentage change in price})}$$

So, for example, if the price of a product (P) rises from $1.00 to $1.10 and as a result the quantity demanded (Q) falls from 1,000 units to 800 units per week, we can determine the elasticity of demand by first calculating the respective percentage changes in both values.

$$\% \text{ change in Q} = 100 \times \frac{(1,000 - 800)}{1,000} = 20$$

$$\% \text{ change in P} = 100 \times \frac{(1.1-1)}{1} = -10$$

Substituting in the above formula for elasticity of demand, we find price elasticity of demand = -2.

Note that although elasticity has a negative value, this is conventionally ignored. If elasticity of demand is greater than one, we say that demand is elastic; if it is less than one, we say that it is inelastic. When demand is elastic, any change in the price of the product leads to a greater-than-proportional change in the quantity demanded. The greater the elasticity of demand, the greater the effect on the quantity demanded that results from a change in price and vice versa.

Anticipating the effect of price changes

Price elasticity is important to firms when they come to implement price changes. If demand is price-elastic, any reduction in price will tend to lead to a rise in total revenue, and any increase in price will tend to lead to a fall in total revenue. Look at the above elasticity calculation and note that in this example demand is elastic. Before the price rise total revenue was $100 x 1,000 = $100,000. After the price rise total revenue fell to $110 x 800 = $88,000.

If demand had been inelastic, the number of units sold would have remained constant regardless of any change in the unit price, thus increasing revenue when price rises. Examples of goods that are price-inelastic are staple foods, such as bread and milk—raising the price of such commodities increases revenue, while reducing it diminishes revenue. In either case, however, the number of units sold will remain constant.

ABOVE: In the United States there are so many competing producers of frankfurters that if one raises its prices, it will lose sales to other firms.

Finance and accounting

All firms and businesses—no matter how large or small—must keep detailed records of all their financial transactions. This is not only so that they can keep up to date with their own profits and losses, but also to comply with legal requirements.

The financial success of a firm is of enormous importance to its owners, directors, employees, and shareholders, and of great significance to potential investors. The only reliable way to determine if a firm is really performing well is by critically examining its accounts. But these documents are by no means straightforward, and the subtleties of a balance sheet take a lot of effort to understand fully. Nevertheless, the study rewards the time invested and is an essential part of success in business.

Assets and liabilities

Most people and virtually all firms have assets and liabilities. An asset may be either something you own—money, land, buildings, goods, trademarks, patents, brand names, shares in other firms—or something that someone else owes you. In other words, something that is rightfully yours but which is currently in someone else's possession.

Such an intangible asset is often money that you are owed for work or goods you have sold and which is due to be paid after the expiration of a previously agreed length of time (a credit period).

A liability is anything you owe to someone else and expect to have to hand over at some time in the future. Liabilities often involve some kind of financial debt that is recorded in the form of a bill.

The balance sheet

The balance sheet is the most basic document in which the performance of a firm is tabulated. A balance sheet is simply a table listing a firm's assets and liabilities together with the value of those assets and liabilities at one moment in time. It is no more than a financial snapshot.

The balance sheet for a teenager shown on page 49 is an extremely simple personal

ABOVE: Making provision for the future can be crucial to the viability of a business. Lack of investment can hinder expansion opportunities, while unforeseen expenses might push it into debt.

A teenager's personal balance sheet

(December 31, 2000)

ASSETS	$
Computer	.500
Stereo	.250
Clothes	.750
Jewelry	.150
Mountain bike	.500
Automobile	.1,000
Total assets	**.3,150**

LIABILITIES	$
Magazine subscriptions	.10
Phone bills	.75
Automobile costs	.100
Software upgrades	.75
Credit card	.150
Bike parts	.100
Total liabilities	**510**

NET WORTH	.$
Inheritance	.2,320
Savings	.320
Total	**.2,640**

ABOVE: Entering accounts in ledgers is a comparatively rare practice these days. Powerful computer software has revolutionized the painstaking task of double-entry bookkeeping for big and small firms alike.

one. Nevertheless, exactly the same principles are applied to the compilation of any such document, and the balance sheet of even the most diverse business corporation does not vary much from this format. It just becomes more complicated as other factors are taken into account.

An important part of the basic balance sheet is the concept of "net." Net means the value of an item after the deduction of something else. The teenager's total assets and total liabilities are listed, and a figure for his net worth is found by deducting those liabilities from assets. So, in the example, net worth is $2,640 ($3,150 minus $510). If you sold off all your assets—an act known as liquidation—and paid off all your liabilities, the amount left over would be your net worth or your net assets.

The final part of the balance sheet gives some indication of how the teenager came to be worth $2,640. He may have been given some of his assets. This is what he "inherited" or started out with. Alternatively, he may have acquired all his money by saving some or all of his earnings. In this scenario "savings" would be deemed to include any asset that may be sold and turned into cash. Any per-sonal spending on food, drink, and vacations is lost forever. Tangible items, on the other hand—computer, clothes, mobile phone, etc.—can always be sold off and are thus categorized as savings.

When you read a firm or a business's balance sheet, there are a number of financial terms that regularly crop up. They are outlined in the box below.

Another example on page 50 shows a fairly standard balance sheet for a small firm. In this the term "Total shareholders' equity" is simply another means of expressing "net worth"—that is, a different way of showing

Financial terms

Fixed assets.

A fixed asset is any asset that a firm uses on a long-term continuing basis, rather than one that is bought to be sold on to customers. Fixed assets include such things as buildings, machinery, vehicles, and computers.

Current assets.

Current assets are assets you anticipate will be sold within one year.

Current liabilities.

Current liabilities are debts you expect to pay within the next year—typically they are money owed to suppliers.

Long-term liabilities.

Long-term liabilities are debts you expect to pay but not within the next year. They include loans from financial institutions.

Fast Eddy's mountain bike emporium

(Balance sheet at January 1, 2001)

ASSETS	$'000s
Fixed assets	.20,500
Current assets	.13,500
Total assets	**.34,000**

LIABILITIES	
Current liabilities	.8,000
Long-term liabilities	.21,000
Total liabilities	**.29,000**

SHAREHOLDERS' EQUITY	
Capital invested	.1,500
Retained profit	.3,500
Total shareholders equity	**.5,000**

the net assets of a business and how they are produced. "Capital invested" is the amount of money put into the firm by shareholders—its owners. "Retained profit" is what the firm has earned or "saved" once suppliers, wages, and taxes have all been paid.

Balancing the books

In its simplest form a firm is no more than a legal framework in which a group of investors or shareholders may organize their investment. And within any firm someone has a claim on every single asset. The someone in question could be an employee, a shareholder, a bank, or a supplier. One way of calculating the shareholders' equity is by subtracting liabilities from assets.

Transactions

A balance sheet is not simply a list of assets and liabilities. It also includes transactions—that is, the exchange or transfer of goods, services and funds. Transactions include raising money from shareholders and banks, the purchase of materials, and payments to staff. Large firms make many thousands of transactions each year, and so need to have computers and separate accounting departments.

Even when all the transactions have been collected together and entered onto a balance sheet, various adjustments have still to be made in order to reflect the true financial position of the firm. They include depreciation and amortization, two important and closely related terms in finance and accounting that are explained below.

Depreciation

Most of the fixed assets of any business diminish in value over the length of time during which they are used in the business. This loss in value—which is known as depreciation—is chargeable against profits made during the working life of the asset concerned. It is standard accounting practice to reduce a fixed asset's value by one-third after its first year of use. Subsequently, the fixed asset is deemed to lose 10 percent a year. Thus, for example, if a firm buys a desk costing $1,500, a year later it will be deemed to be worth $1,000. At the end of year two its book value will be $900, and at the end of year three it will be worth 90 percent of $900—$810. Even if it is an antique that in fact increases in value each year, in accounting terms it will still be written down by the same percentage annually. If the asset is an exhaustible natural resource, its loss in value is known as depletion.

Amortization

If a business buys a long lease on its premises, the principle of depreciation is the same as above, but the term amortization is used to describe it since the lease is dying away with each passing year—*mort* is the French word for death. If, for example, a lease on a building is bought for $10,000, and the length of the lease is 10 years, then one tenth, or $1,000, will be written off each year.

Businesses can make money from their property. In boom times property values escalate. Consequently, there is often a shortage of suitable business space, and firms can sell leases in prime locations at a profit.

LEFT: An original stock certificate of the Ford Motor Company issued in 1903. Henry Ford's own stake in the company was 255 shares, worth $100 each.

Dividends

These days big businesses that would once have owned the buildings in which their operations are based now sell them and then lease the buildings back from the new owners. The advantage of this tactic is that it enables firms to take the money gained from selling an office or factory and reinvest it in their core activities. Alternatively, they can return the proceeds to shareholders in the form of an enlarged dividend. This sale-and-leaseback device has been widely used in recent times by Microsoft and IBM, two computer giants that desire the greater liquidity thus provided.

A dividend is defined as the amount of money per share that a firm pays to its shareholders at the end of each financial year. It is usually expressed either as a percentage of the nominal value of the share or as an absolute amount per share. Take for example a firm that has issued capital of $500,000 in the form of 500,000 ordinary $1 shares—if the directors decide to distribute $25,000, they would thus be said to be declaring a dividend of 5 percent or 5 cents per share.

Some large U.S. firms pay dividends quarterly or four times a year. That is because the shareowning culture is so strong in the United States that firms have to provide incentives, in the form of dividends, to those who have invested in them. The alternative would be to run the risk of shareholders taking their money out of the firm and investing it elsewhere—worst of all, with firms that are in direct competition.

Increased dividends are generally regarded as a sign of economic good times. However, the payment of dividends naturally reduces the overall profitability of a firm and gives away money that might be better reinvested. On the other hand, healthy dividends may make a firm more attractive to new investors.

LEFT: Office buildings in downtown Los Angeles. Property leases might be a firm's most valuable asset, particularly in areas where there is a shortage of business space.

Basic concepts of accounting

Accountants generally take a pessimistic view of life and are sometimes accused of being boring. They are often prudent and cautious by nature. They are wise to be like this. If there is a possibility that a customer may not pay for the goods that he or she has bought, accountants make a provision against it. This means a reduction in the retained profit of the affected firm. Businesspeople may object, but an accountant will remain unshakeably convinced that it is "the prudent thing to do."

There are many ways of presenting accounts. But a firm that has adopted one method should stick with it. Consistency is important, otherwise analysts cannot take a long-term view of a firm.

Keeping business records

There are many excellent reasons why a firm should keep accurate, easily accessible, and well-presented business records. The tax man requires it, and bank managers need regular and reliable information about a business's health.

Accounts are kept in several books. The cash book is the most basic book. It records all payments and receipts made by check or in cash. Some businesses are purely cash ones—this means that regardless of whether a particular transaction is a purchase or a sale, payment is made immediately.

Other businesses that buy and sell with payment at a later date need two further books—a sales day book for recording sales invoices as they are sent out, and a purchases day book in which are recorded all acquisitions of goods and services.

As businesses expand, they start keeping sales ledgers that record the individual accounts of all their customers. Using a sales ledger, a business can tell which customers are late payers and which customers place substantial orders. Similarly, a purchase day book should be kept. It is ruled with a number of vertical columns in which different kinds of expenditure are registered. By adding to these columns each month, a business can see exactly what its costs are.

Double-entry bookkeeping

The double-entry of business transactions on an account or balance sheet puts into practice the fundamental principle of accounting. This principle states that assets must always equal claims against those assets. In short, the balance sheet has to balance. This is because of property rights, and the importance of keeping track of the financing and ownership of

assets acquired in the operation of a business. Somebody must own each resource used by a business or firm. Balancing the books or balance sheets is just a way to ensure that ownership of everything in the firm has been accounted for.

In essence, double-entry bookkeeping means that every transaction is recorded twice in a different part of the accounts. For every debit there must be a corresponding credit, traditionally on opposite pages of the ledger book. The double-entry method was first used in 15th-century Italy as a way of ensuring that accounts represented an accurate picture of a firm's financial position.

In order to illustrate the practical operation of double-entry book-keeping, imagine that you are the owner of an on-line flower business called flowers.com. To expand flowers.com, you buy an extra delivery van. Once the purchase is made, your accountant makes two entries on flowers.com's accounts. Say the van cost $6,000. An entry would be made

ABOVE: Accountants may be naturally cautious, but their careful assessment of cash flow and expenses is key to a firm's overall profitability.

in the cash payment section of flowers.com's balance sheet. But once you have bought your van, it also becomes an asset worth exactly $6,000 and is entered as such. This is the essence of all double-entry bookkeeping. The principle is simple, but there are two important things to remember. One is that any payment by your business that results in money leaving its bank account immediately is regarded as a cash payment. You may have bought that delivery van using a check, but even so, it still qualifies as a cash payment. The other thing to remember is that flowers.com's new asset—the van—will now depreciate in value on an annual basis as outlined above.

Accruals

Accruals are any costs for which you have not been billed but for which you know you will have to pay. For instance, faulty administration at a telephone firm may mean that you do not receive a phone bill for six months. But when that bill arrives, it is likely to be a hefty one. Such an enlarged bill would be included in the accruals section of a firm's balance sheet. Similarly, the accruals basis of accounting may include sales a firm has made but that have not yet been paid for. All the costs in making those sales have to be included in an account or balance sheet as well.

Profit and loss (P&L)

A firm's profitability tells the analyst something about a firm, but it does not give the whole picture of its health and wealth. It is just the headline figure. For a comprehensive

understanding of how a firm makes its money the profit-and-loss account section (P&L) in a balance sheet is required reading. The P&L breaks down all the major sales transactions that contributed money or profits to the business. It also shows which items cost the firm money.

Cash flow

It is possible for a firm to make a good profit during a year of trading and yet be short of cash. This could be because considerable investment has been channeled into stock for the business, or it could be that the accrual basis of accounting shows that stock has been sold, but payment for it has yet to be received. As a result, a business may have a poor cash flow. Unless careful plans have been made to acquire financial investment and cover late payments, a business may find it hard to survive because it needs funds to cover day-to-day expenses. Day-to-day expenses include loan obligations and the payment of creditors.

Venture capitalists (investors who are willing to take a risk on a new business in exchange for a say in how the company is run and a share of the profits) or banks that are considering lending money to start up new businesses will demand a cash-flow forecast before they commit to investment funding. The principle of cash-flow forecasting is very straightforward. It is simply a prediction of the future sales of a firm minus its expected overheads and costs.

Every business has a break-even point at which it is producing just enough for the receipts to balance the costs. Before this point

ABOVE: Stock bought for this flower shop may have required a cash outlay, but it can now be regarded as an asset of the firm.

ABOVE: *Governments have to keep accounts of income and expenditure from taxes and state programs. Here, President Clinton announces a $20 billion federal budget surplus on projections for the fiscal year 1999.*

is reached, the business is working at a loss; when this point is passed, the business shows a profit. The firm's success is measured by the amount of profit that it earns.

Sometimes a one-time event will cause a firm to earn income or incur expenses that it would not expect in the ordinary course of its business, and that it does not expect to recur. The income or expense resulting from such an event is known as an extraordinary item. Extraordinary items can include money paid out in damages through the loss of a legal case. Many firms incur extraordinary losses if they refinance their loans through a new lender who offers a cheaper rate of interest than the original provider of funding. The penalty incurred by changing their financing is charged on a balance sheet as an extraordinary item.

Financial terminology

The following terms are some of those most commonly used in finance and accounting:
● Earnings per share (EPS) is a method used by investors and analysts to make valuations of a firm. The figure is often shown in the last line of the profit-and-loss account on a balance sheet. EPS equals profits for the year divided by the number of firm shares in existence.
● Return on capital employed (ROCE) is usually defined as the net profit after depreciation as a percentage of the average capital invested in a business. It is one of a number of

financial ratios used to measure the efficiency of a business or the efficiency of a particular investment project, and is also known as the rate of return.

To calculate ROCE, the operating profit of a firm (the amount of money a business makes before the payment of tax and debts) is divided by the financial capital employed within the business, which can sometimes exclude loans and working capital.

Prospective investors may compare the ROCE of a firm with the percentage return they would get on an ordinary savings account. ROCE should be higher. If it is not, the business will not appeal to prospective investors. It is also desirable from the investors' point of view that ROCE should increase over a period of time.
● The rate of return is the annual rate of growth of an investment or portfolio. It may be announced in anticipation of an expected rate of return, or it can be reported retrospectively as an experienced rate of return. The rate of return is calculated using the following equation, where T = years and V_O and V_t are the initial and final market values of the investment respectively:

$$(V_t/V_O) \times \frac{1}{T} - 1$$

An investment of $100 that grows to $109 over a year has a rate of return of 9 percent. In the following year, if the full $109 is left in the firm and there is again a growth rate of 9 percent, this rate of interest will accrue on the whole amount—the original $100 investment plus the first year's interest. Interest in year two will therefore be:

$$109 + \frac{(109 \times 9)}{100} = \$118.81$$

This is compound interest, which builds up on a daily basis but is normally calculated and reported annually. Occasionally, however, the rate of return will be reported more frequently. For instance, in the fast-moving and volatile NASDAQ new technology stock market, share gains in a specific firm can be so great that returns of interest are calculated by fund managers every three months.

When the term "return" is used on its own, it can mean several things. Usually, it refers to the total return, which is the total value of an investment on a specified date—this includes principal income and capital gains. The total return may also be expressed as a percentage. For example, if $50 were invested for a year and in that time returned $60, it would be said to have a 120 percent total return.

● A firm's price to earnings ratio (P/E) is the price of a stock divided by its earnings per share. This ratio gives an investor an idea of how much he or she is paying for a particular firm's earning power. It is thus one of the most fundamental measures of a firm's value.

The P/E is determined by dividing the price of the stock by the firm's earnings per share. For example, if the stock of a firm has a closing price of $15 per share and the firm's earnings per share is $1.50, the P/E ratio is 10.

Investors use the P/E multiple to help them choose which firms are likely to prove the best investments. Firms with a P/E multiple of less than 10 are considered low-growth firms. This may be because these firms are in low-growth industries, in a sector that has fallen out of favor, or because they are established blue-chip firms with long records of earnings stability and high dividends.

Firms with a P/E over 15 are considered dynamic. Such firms often have low income and may pay out no dividend, preferring instead to reinvest the profits they make in research and development or new machinery and technology. A high P/E multiple reflects the future growth potential of a firm. Nevertheless, it should be noted that for all its significance, a P/E is not an absolute measure of a firm's value.

● The internal rate of return (IRR)—also known as the average annual total return—is the rate at which the present value of an investment's future cash flows equals the cost of investment. The IRR is similar to the interest rate on a savings account—that is, its value is the interest rate the savings account pays to give you the same return on your investment throughout the same time frame.

BELOW: Monitors at the NASDAQ stock exchange. Share prices can move up or down rapidly depending on general market fluctuations or confidence in a particular firm's business performance.

● Book value is the value that an item has on the balance sheet—literally, in the books. Items may be of more value to a firm than to someone in the outside world, which is why the market value and book value of an item may not correspond.

● Overtrading is the problem of a firm that has too little capital to carry its turnover with safety given its present policies. For example, a firm might double its production but then find it cannot meet its current expenditures because too much capital is now tied up. If the situation is not remedied, the firm risks going bankrupt. Overtrading can always be avoided by sacrificing profit to liquidity in some way. Overtrading can only be justified in small, fast-growing firms or for short periods in other firms. It must always be deliberate and under tight control.

Funding a business

Businesses raise money in a number of ways. They can take out a loan with a bank or use an overdraft. Other options include selling equity or shares to raise cash. When a firm is public, it can sell bonds. A bond is a way of raising money that can be traded on the financial markets. The firm borrows and promises to repay the loan at a fixed rate of interest over a certain period. The loan is normally secured on the firm's assets—that is to say, the lender will have the security of knowing that if the debt is not repaid, it will be able to seize the firm's goods to the value of the outstanding amount. Convertible bonds permit the lender to convert the bonds into ordinary shares.

Debt-to-capital ratio

Ignoring tax to be paid, the total funding of a business is the sum of the debt and the money invested in it—its equity. The debt-to-total-capital ratio is the debt divided by the total funding. The higher the percentage, the more the firm relies on borrowing to survive.

Borrowing is fine in a low-interest-rate climate, when the cost of money is relatively cheap. But if the prospect of price rises (inflation) causes the Federal Reserve to increase interest rates, which in turn raise the cost of bank borrowing, firms can be vulnerable because they cannot pay off (service) their debts.

The term "leveraging" is used generally to describe the concept of borrowing money in pursuit of investment returns.

Taxation

The tax laws of each nation are usually unique to it, although there are similarities and common elements in the laws of various countries. The growth of international con-

tacts means that a corporation may be taxed in several countries. Various international agreements are designed to prevent double taxation either by defining the application of the tax laws of each nation or by providing for credits in each country for taxes paid under the legislation of the other.

In the United States the taxation of businesses to raise money for federal or state coffers is an extremely complicated area. It is also an area prone to rapid changes if legislators decide to shift tax thresholds or to impose restrictions on individual business sectors. Most people in business, whether they are self-employed or run large corporations, retain a tax adviser or accountant to navigate them through this minefield.

There are countless rules on expenses, assets, and profits. Consequently, it is very hard for unqualified people to keep abreast of the latest tax regulations. Accountants typically charge from $400 to fill in a tax return for a self-employed business. Firms usually spend the money: good accountants are invaluable. The amount of money they should save a business ought to dwarf their fees.

The profits of any business—no matter whether it be a sole proprietor, a partnership, or a firm—are computed by taking profits

ABOVE: Three brass balls, symbol of a pawnbroking firm in the United Kingdom. They advance cash to customers against goods held as security, making their own profit from interest on the loan or by selling unredeemed items.

according to a firm's accounts and then adjusting it. The adjustment is necessary because the normal rules for preparing a set of accounts are not the same as in tax law. Accounting profit will often bear very little relation to taxable profit. This is because a range of expenses and tax-deductible items can reduce a tax bill by hundreds, even thousands of dollars.

An accountant's help is vital here if you do not wish to pay more tax than you are legally obliged to. Having said that, it pays to keep abreast of all the latest financial and taxation rules announced by politicians in federal and state budget statements. The business pages of good newspapers also break down the latest information into a readily understandable form.

You are allowed to charge an expense against your income if it is:
● incurred wholly and exclusively for the purpose of trade;
● properly charged against income (not for example, purchase of a property lease, which is categorized as capital);
● not specifically disallowed by law.

Ways to save tax

There is not the space to list all the expenses that are allowable. But the following are useful pointers.
● If you do some of your work from home, you can normally charge a proportion of your rent, light, heat, and telephone bills against your business income.
● In some states, if you get married and your wife cannot work outside the home because, for instance, she may be looking after young children, she can qualify as an employee and be paid a wage that will be deducted from your profits but not be taxable.
● Records of all research, stationery, and entertainment expenses should also be kept since they, together with travel for the purpose of business, are tax deductible. This means that a portion of your expenses, normally about 25 percent of your tax-deductible items, can be offset against any profits you may have made. This makes your final tax bill much smaller than it would otherwise have been.
● If you work for yourself, it is vital to keep all your invoices and records of payment in date order in clearly marked files. Past records should be kept for a set number of years before they can be discarded.

The financial year

In the United States sole proprietors have to file their tax returns at the beginning of the calendar year. Corporations can choose when their financial year begins and ends. Most

retailers choose to report their financial statements and file their tax returns at the beginning of the calendar year, which is traditionally one of the quietest times. The U.S. federal government makes its main financial statement on or around September 30 each year.

When it comes to taxation, the biggest difference in treatment between sole proprietors, partnerships, and corporations relates to the approach to losses. If a person is running their business as a sole proprietor or partnership, their business income is regarded as just one of their sources of income. That is why losses can be offset against tax.

However, since a corporation is regarded as a separate legal entity, the firm has its own tax liability. This means that the owners cannot set firm losses against their other income. If you are the chief executive officer (CEO) of a corporation, you have to pay taxes under pay-as-you-earn (PAYE) provisions. Consequently, the CEOs' tax burden will be heavier than if they were self-employed. Unless all the profit is taken out of a corporation as executive's pay, the balance will be subject to corporation tax.

ABOVE: Decisions on interest rates by the U.S. Federal Reserve Bank can have a significant effect on a firm's ability to pay its debts.

Auditing

Auditing is the independent examination of an organization's accounts to verify their truth and accuracy. The practice can be traced back to ancient times, but formal auditing as it exists today was established in the latter part of the 19th century. During this period technology in western Europe and the United States evolved rapidly from old-fashioned hand methods to mechanized factories. It required increased financing to achieve this. Early businesses were financed by either a sole proprietor or a partnership. As a result, credit was limited to what the owners themselves could provide.

The rise of joint stock firms increased the possibility of raising capital for industry. Joint stock firms involved a broadening of the shareholding base of a specific firm to encourage more money into the business.

The liability of each shareholder was limited—this meant that if the firm failed, the shareholders would not have to pay all the outstanding debts. Thus it became possible to offer shares to the public, and in this way a vast new supply of capital became available to industry and commerce. Giant industrial businesses with a wide body of shareholders largely took the place of the small, privately owned businesses.

Under this form of organization the shareholders as a body delegate the management of a business to a board of executives. Periodically the board submits to the shareholders the accounts of the firm so that the shareholders can see its financial position.

While the executives of a firm are responsible for presenting the accounts, an objective view is still needed. It was impossible for each individual shareholder to inspect independently a firm's books, so auditors would be appointed to verify a firm's financial situation and approve its methods of accounting. Auditors, who are trained accountants, have a statutory duty to make a critical review of the accounts submitted by the executives and to report to the shareholders whether those accounts represent a true and fair view and comply with financial legislation.

If the auditors disagree with a firm's interpretation of its accounts, it is their duty to say so and in their report to specify what aspects they disagree with. Auditors picking holes in a firm's accounts is not justification for their replacement unless the shareholders of the firm in question no longer have confidence in them. Usually the onus is on the firm to justify its account procedures and clarify its business situation.

Confidence between company executives and auditors is desirable, but it is not totally necessary for the satisfactory performance

of auditors. Indeed, it is often inevitable that auditors and a firm's executives will clash. Auditors of public firms are appointed and paid by shareholders, although shareholders often delegate to executives the power to set the auditors' remuneration.

When undertaking an audit, accountants must work in accordance with the generally accepted accounting principles (GAAP). These standards are made public by the Auditing Standards Board—an arm of the American Institute of Certified Public Accountants (AICPA). The auditor's report or opinion will appear in the firm's annual report and will also be filed with the Securities and Exchange Commission (SEC).

Liability laws

Many smaller accounting firms are unwilling to perform audits because they fear being sued for inaccurate or incorrect information and negligence. In 1990 Laventhol & Horwath, then the seventh largest accountants in the United States, declared bankruptcy as a result of mounting litigation costs.

Along with a large body of U.S. corporations, the Big Five U.S. firms—Arthur Andersen, Deloitte & Touche, Ernst & Young, KPMG Peat Marwick, and Price Waterhouse Coopers—have been seeking reform of the liability laws in the United States. In 1995 they achieved some success at the federal level with the passing of securities legislation, but state liability laws continue to be a problem.

Liability: partnerships and limited firms

Many businesses grow from sole proprietors into partnerships or private firms, then eventually expand to become listed firms or pub-

ABOVE: The Wall Street Journal *is one of a number of publications that provides financial information on businesses around the world.*

Auditors' reports

The major types of auditors' reports are:

Unqualified opinion The auditor finds that the financial statements are an accurate reflection of the firm's position and operations as specified by the generally accepted accounting principles (GAAP). Since firms normally work in close concert with their auditors to ensure their procedures are sound, this is the most common type of audit report. Sometimes this audit is alternatively known as a "clean opinion."

Qualified opinion The auditor includes a particular limitation: objective or independent evidence of a particular transaction or policy. The issue causing the qualification must be communicated clearly in the auditor's opinion.

Adverse opinion The auditor issues an unfavorable report. The firm has not issued its financial statements according to GAAP provisions. Adverse opinions are rare, and the auditor must reveal the conditions that led to these conclusions in the audit report.

Disclaimer of opinion The auditor cannot give an opinion usually because he or she cannot complete the audit. This may happen if records are unavailable and cannot be pieced together.

ABOVE: Investigations into the collapse of Robert Maxwell's media empire revealed he had manipulated business accounts to move money between different companies and give a false impression of their worth.

lic corporations. If a business fails, those involved in it have varying degrees of liability depending on the constitution of the particular company (*see* An introduction to business, page 6).

A sole proprietor is a business organization with only one owner. It may be a one-person operation or a large enterprise with many employees. The owner receives all the profits but is also liable to repay debts should the firm go out of business.

Two or more people joining together in business with a view to profit constitute a partnership. Partnerships are more likely to be able to raise money to invest in the business. Partners with complementary skills can work together effectively to the benefit of the firm. Partnerships are traditionally found in the professions: law, accounting, architecture, dentistry, and medicine.

Partners within a practice share all their profits but are also liable to service losses and, in extreme cases, may have to shoulder the burden of debt should the practice go bankrupt. If a partnership breaks up or goes

bankrupt, this can expose individual partners to the risk of paying for mistakes by the other partners. This is why partnerships are often family concerns.

A corporation is a business whose identity in the eyes of the law is separate from its owners. The owners of a corporation are shareholders. Every limited liability firm must have a board of executives, a company secretary, and shareholders to whom it issues shares or equities.

From the shareholders' point of view the attraction of limited liability is that it enables investors to provide capital without those investors running the risk of being held responsible for any subsequent losses. Although people who buy shares may lose the whole of their original contribution, for them this is the worst scenario. Shareholders cannot be forced to pay creditors and make good any business losses by, for example, having to sell their home. Their risk is therefore strictly limited, and they will not be held responsible for the catastrophic losses that may result when a company collapses.

Bankruptcy

A business that cannot pay its debts is considered insolvent and bankrupt in the eyes of the law. Thousands of businesses go bankrupt in the United States every year. Although there is a stigma about a business failing because of its inability to pay its debts, bankruptcy itself is no disgrace. Businesses are often unable to control their own destinies. For instance, they can be vulnerable to economic recessions that result in orders for goods and services diminishing. During the most recent major economic recession at the end of the 1980s the economy in major world nations shrank and bankrupted thousands of firms. This in turn created huge levels of unemployment.

Sometimes a bankruptcy chain can be created. If a major firm goes out of business, its regular suppliers often go down with it since they have no other businesses with which to work. Late payment of bills by big firms can often send smaller businesses "to the wall." If a major business relocates to another area in which wages may be cheaper, a whole region may see firms going bankrupt. Alternatively, firms can go bust if they expand too quickly or make bad business decisions.

Bankruptcy began as a creditor's remedy to claw back through the courts debts that otherwise seemed impossible to collect. In former times bankrupts were considered to be defrauders and criminals, and were punished socially and professionally; some were even required to wear a degrading form of dress. In Victorian Britain during the 19th century bankrupts were thrown into debtors' jail as punishment for not paying creditors the money they owed them. The trouble with this punishment code was that it left creditors still without their money and gave the debtors no chance to pay it back. Gradually, governments realized that imprisonment made the situation worse. Eventually, bankruptcy evolved into a source of relief for debtors from financial distress, and procedures were put in place to give creditors a chance to recoup some of their losses.

Bankruptcy in the United States is regulated by the Bankruptcy Reform Act (BRA) of 1978. The BRA, often referred to as "the code," has been amended on several occasions since 1978. Among the most important alterations were those effected by the "consumer credit" amendments enacted in 1984.

The BRA is supplemented by Bankruptcy Rules. There are also a number of official forms and procedures that must be used by debtors, creditors, and any others wishing to participate in bankruptcy proceedings.

Today, bankruptcy law allows for four types of proceedings. The most common is a Chapter Seven or a liquidation bankruptcy. Under the terms of a Chapter Seven a trustee—normally an accountant who has been given powers of administration over a

ABOVE: Trials for business fraud can be long and complicated, and often require detailed explanation of financial documents to the jury. It can sometimes take years to prepare a case for court.

bankrupt firm—gathers all the debtor's assets that have not been exempted by state or federal law. He or she then distributes them to pay off debts.

Secured creditors must be satisfied "off the top"—this means that they get dollar for dollar on their claims. Secured creditors are people who lend money to a business on the basis that they can even seize certain assets from a business or a business executive. Such assets will often includes an executive's home. To avoid having their homes taken in the event of bankruptcy, businessmen and women often sign over their property to their spouses or family members prior to getting into difficulty.

Next in line are priority claims. They include administrative expenses associated with the bankruptcy and other special claims such as outstanding taxes and the wages of employees. However, it is important to remember that paying employees once a firm fails is not considered a top priority. There are many cases in which workers have not been paid the wages owed to them following the collapse of a business.

Finally, the claims of unsecured, non-priority claims share whatever assets may remain. They include the customers of a business. Often there will be little money left once prior claims have been settled. So, for example, suppose a firm selling package vacations collapses; customers who have paid money to

that firm are by no means guaranteed to get a vacation or their money returned. Normally there is no differentiation between foreign and domestic creditors, as long as there is a reciprocal agreement between the countries of the parties concerned.

However much (or little) creditors receive in a bankruptcy, a debtor is usually entitled to a discharge. A discharge relieves a debtor of responsibility for most debts existing on the date the petition is filed. Certain debts, such as those for alimony, most student loan obligations, and certain types of personal injury, are excepted from the discharge.

In rare circumstances, such as when the debtor has committed a "bankruptcy crime," the debtor may be denied a discharge. The discharge is the law's embodiment of probably the most important purpose of bankruptcy in the modern world, namely, to give the debtor a "fresh start" financially.

Bankruptcy is started with a petition. The vast majority of cases are begun by the debtor, who files a voluntary petition. It is possible, however, for the debtor to be forced into bankruptcy by creditors who file an involuntary petition. Under the Bankruptcy Reform Act a debtor has certain duties and must file various schedules and lists. They include a list of creditors, a schedule of assets and liabilities, a schedule of current income and expenditures, and a statement of financial affairs.

ABOVE: *Penalties for debt were harsh in 19th-century Britain. Offenders were sometimes hanged in front of what became known as the "Debtor's Door" at London's Newgate prison.*

Competition, expansion, and growth

One of the most fascinating aspects of economics is the study of the ways in which firms compete with each other for a share of the market. It is also one of the most complicated.

Firms and businesses exist in a variety of different forms, from sole proprietorships to partnerships and large multinational corporations. Similarly, they might be privately owned by one person, by a small group of partners, or by thousands of shareholders around the world. Firms face different market conditions and have different goals—most are profit maximizers, but some businesses are more concerned with maximizing sales revenue or (in the case of charities) simply looking to cover their costs.

The firm way forward

For most firms in free-market and mixed economies, however, no matter what their size, structure, or ownership, the only way forward is through profit maximization. And for most firms this goal can be achieved only by competing with other, similar firms that sell similar goods and services. These firms operate within a market. The market mechanism decides what should be produced, and only those willing and able to pay the market price for those products and services will become consumers.

Within the market the assumption made by economists is that completely free competition will be in the best interests of both consumers and suppliers.

Firms may grow in two ways—either by increasing their output, revenues, and profitability, or through amalgamation, merger, or takeover. Amalgamations and mergers take place with the consent of all parties—the heads of both firms agree to the link-ups and work together to make them succeed. We will look at the different types of merger in greater detail below (*see* page 73).

There are times when everyone involved agrees to a takeover, but at other times such a move may be resisted by the firm that has been targeted. In cases such as this—which are known as hostile takeover bids—the directors of the firm under threat will advise and encourage their shareholders to reject the offer made for their shares by the new firm (the

prospective buyer needs to acquire just over 50 percent of the shares in order to take control of the firm.)

Competitive markets

The conditions for free or perfect competition are that there should be a large number of producers and consumers of a good, that there should be free entry to and exit from the market, that there should be perfect information, and that goods should be homogeneous. It is also assumed that firms aim to maximize profits. According to most economists, if all these conditions are satisfied, resources will be allocated efficiently, and goods and services will be produced and supplied to the maximum benefit of all (*see* box opposite).

Under the conditions of perfect competition firms and businesses compete with each other on the basis of price and quantity of the good they are producing. An equilibrium—or market-

ABOVE: The worst case scenario. Like great white sharks, firms must go forward or die. Unlike the killer fish, however, the firm's interests may also be to the benefit of society as a whole.

The QWERTY keyboard

ABOVE: The order of letters on the typewriter keyboard is now universally standard—but is it the best arrangement?

Economists assume that free competition will result in the production and supply of products that are exactly what people want in terms of price, quality, and quantity, and that such competition will encourage the production of technologically advanced and efficient products given the available resources. In order to test the accuracy of this assumption, economists have tried to find situations in which the market has made a mistake, and the resulting product is not as technologically advanced, or effective, as it could be. If such examples can be found, there might be an argument for using some other mechanism—that is, a mechanism other than the market—for allocating resources or for there to be some kind of intervention into the market by government.

Designed not to jam

The QWERTY typewriter keyboard is sometimes given as an example of the market making a mistake, resulting in a product and technology that are arguably inferior to what might have been produced had there been some kind of government intervention. In 1868 Christopher Soles patented the QWERTY design keyboard—so named for the first group of letters at the top of the keyboard. This design and layout of the keyboard supposedly solved the problem of bars jamming when certain combinations of typewriter keys were struck. A different layout,

patented by Dvorak in 1936, was then introduced. It was supposed to be a superior and more efficient design. However, despite the recoverability of retraining costs, typists refused to move to the new design. Nor would manufacturers adopt and produce the new Dvorak keyboard.

The inefficient design appeared to be "locked in"—that is, neither consumers nor producers would consider adopting the apparently superior technology. It has been argued that this gives an example of a coordination failure—the market had failed to reach the most efficient outcome.

In 1991 economists S. Margolis and S. Liebowitz suggested that the popular arguments about efficiency in this case were doubtful. The main study supporting the Dvorak keyboard—a report which claimed that it was a superior layout for a typewriting keyboard—was undertaken by the U.S. Navy in 1944. Margolis and Liebowitz challenged this report on the grounds of statistical theory and pointed out that the report was organized by Lieutenant-Commander August Dvorak, who was also the owner of the Dvorak patent. Later studies in 1956 by the U.S. General Services Administration had tended to confirm that there was little to choose between the two keyboards in terms of efficiency and speed. If the QWERTY design was actually as efficient as the Dvorak design, then the market did not fail in this case after all.

clearing—price is reached when the quantity produced and sold by suppliers is equal to the quantity demanded and bought by consumers (*see* page 28, How a business works).

In the real world, for a variety of reasons the best outcome may not always be achieved, and the market mechanism is said to have failed. Firms exist in markets that range from conditions of almost perfect competition to monopoly. A combination of monopoly power, externalities, absence of property rights, and information asymmetries can result in inefficient market outcomes. These present themselves in two forms: failure to achieve the efficient distribution of resources (*see* page 100, Market failure and externalities), and failure to serve some social goal, such as income distribution.

The possibility that markets can result in outcomes that are inefficient or sociably undesirable raises the question of intervention by outside authorities such as the government.

Nonprice competition

Classical economic theory analyzes markets in terms of price and quantity. In the real world, however, the conditions for perfect competition are seldom met. This imperfection enables firms and businesses to compete with each other not only on a price basis but also by a method known as nonprice competition. Techniques of attracting or trying to attract business away from competitors include advertising and product differentiation.

Product differentiation involves distinguishing what are essentially the same or very similar products or goods by real or illusory methods. Among the products that may be distinguished in this way are breakfast cereals, detergents, and gasoline. Products might be exactly the same, but they are differentiated through distinctive packaging, or persuasive advertising that may convince consumers to buy a particular brand rather than that of a rival (*see* Branding, page 67).

In cases of this type we need not assume that products are homogeneous, as they would be under perfect competition. Although one detergent may be essentially the same as another, consumers may perceive it as being different from or superior to the competition. Thus product differentiation allows firms to increase the price of their product without necessarily losing sales because brand loyalty leads purchasers to stick with the brand they know.

On a more positive note, however, firms may choose to differentiate their products through actual improvements in quality or performance, thus encouraging technological innovation. So, for example, lead-free gas is distinguished from leaded gas because the former is less polluting and damaging to the environment and human health. Similarly, rechargable batteries, while more expensive than ordinary batteries, are marketed on the basis that they have a longer life and can be used again and again. This not only benefits consumers but also results in fewer batteries being thrown away.

Nonprice competition is most common in markets where there is some kind of oligopoly power—that is, markets that are dominated by a few large suppliers (*see* page 80, How firms behave in the real world). In these situations price cutting can lead to damaging price wars, so firms all set the same price and prefer to compete through the use of special offers, free gifts, competitions, and often expensive marketing campaigns.

BELOW: If one breakfast cereal is very much like another, each manufacturer has to suggest differences that are perceived rather than real. Shredded Wheat may be good to eat, but in what sense is it "national"?

THE NATIONAL BREAKFAST

(as you eat it in Strawberry time)

● Wake up those lagging appetites. It's strawberry time! Heap a handful of luscious, juicy berries over golden-brown Shredded Wheat. Add rich, wholesome milk and a sprinkling of sugar. *It's the National Breakfast!* . . . Shredded Wheat is the national favorite for its crisp, chewy flavor. But still more important, it's packed with vigorous health and energy....Whole wheat, you know,

is Mother Nature's favorite. To this golden grain she gave her most abundant array of the vital elements that build strong bones, muscle and vigor. *And Shredded Wheat is whole wheat!*— nothing added, nothing taken away—made of the choicest, plumpest, sun-ripened grains, selected from the nation's richest harvest fields . . . Try this national favorite tomorrow morning.

The **NATIONAL** *Breakfast*
Because—Shredded Wheat with milk is the most delicious, satisfying breakfast you can eat. *Because* —it contains the health-building elements the body needs—bran, mineral salts, calcium, carbohydrates, proteins, vitamins, phosphorus and iron. Ask for the package showing the picture of Niagara Falls and the red N.B.C. Uneeda Seal.

SHREDDED WHEAT

A Product of NATIONAL BISCUIT COMPANY **"Uneeda Bakers"**

LEFT: Banks may attract new customers by offering a larger network of ATMs than their rivals—this is an example of nonprice competition.

There are many examples of nonprice competition. Banks, for instance, find it very limiting to engage in price competition. That is because they have only restricted powers of discretion (partly because of government regulation) to alter the interest rates on different types of accounts. Instead, they enhance competition through the development of services such as check cards, debit cards, and ATMs. More recent developments include telephone banking and Internet banking. One bank will develop a new facility; but if it is a success, it will rapidly be emulated by its competitors, and so the search for new ways to attract customers continues. For example, consumers may be persuaded to change their bank or their credit card not because they will earn higher rates of interest on their money, but because of an offer—a free flight, say, or a pocket calculator. Some nonprice competition achieves its objective through offering no more than the possibility of a bonus: "Take out credit card X today and earn a chance to win the vacation of a lifetime in our prize drawing."

Spreadsheets and nonprice competition

The development of spreadsheet software also provides many examples of nonprice competition. The electronic spreadsheet was first developed by Bricklin and Frankston, who created VisiCalc for the Apple II. In 1982 an article on spreadsheet software in *Personal Computing* magazine listed 18 spreadsheets in existence, most of which ran on the Apple II or on microcomputers using an operating system called CP/M. Then, in 1983 Lotus introduced the Lotus 1-2-3 spreadsheet at a cost of $495. The Lotus software was immediately recognized as being a superior product to that produced by VisiCalc. At the time it was described as "state of the art" by *PC World* magazine. A year later Lotus 1-2-3 was outselling

LEFT: Spreadsheets are at the cutting edge of a highly competitive market in computer software in which the consumer has high expectations and a wide range of choice.

VisiCalc; VisiCalc was taken off the market in 1985. Lotus had successfully competed with Bricklin and Frankston on the basis of the superior technology they developed.

In general, a lower-quality and lower-priced product would be expected to have a larger market share than a higher-quality, higher-priced product. So, for example, a company such as Ford sells more family cars than Mercedes sells luxury vehicles. At any one time in the spreadsheet software market, however, most spreadsheet programs are priced very similarly to competing spreadsheet software.

The pricing of spreadsheets is a complex story. The retail price does not really reflect the true average price of the product.

Economists undertook a detailed comparison of the average costs of Lotus and Excel spreadsheet software and the prices received for them by the manufacturers. Excel, introduced by Microsoft, was the first Windows spreadsheet. It was also part of an excellent office suite. This comparison took into account lower upgrade prices, the prices charged for software sold in office suite packages, and discounts granted to trade sources. They found little difference between prices for the two. It was not until 1996 that Lotus 1-2-3 dropped its price sharply in comparison with Excel's, a move that was made only after its market share had fallen below that of Excel.

Although price is an important factor in competition, clearly in the spreadsheet market (as in many other markets) there were other forces at work. Microsoft, with its Excel software, gambled on Windows becoming the predominant operating system. An operating system is like a management device. It controls all the actions of the computer and tells other software how and when to perform its functions. Lotus, meanwhile, was concerned that it was losing market share in the DOS market. DOS was the operating system that PCs used before Windows. Lotus, gambling on the DOS system remaining dominant, decided to produce another version of 1-2-3 that was for the DOS market. As users moved away from DOS to Windows, Lotus's market share plummeted.

In this case nonprice factors were determining the market share of both firms. A marketing mistake had been made by Lotus when it gambled on the wrong operating system dominating the future market; Microsoft, meanwhile, took a chance on new technology coming to lead the market, and the gamble paid off. Although Lotus had been the king of spreadsheets, it has now all but disappeared from the world's computer screens.

After-sales service

After-sales service is another method used by firms in nonprice competition. The word-processor software WordPerfect 5.1 illustrates how this concept has been used in the information technology (IT) industry. WordPerfect dominated the word-processing market in the early 1990s; most people with a PC used this form of software. Still, many found WordPerfect difficult to use, with many awkward features. Microsoft Word was a major alternative, but this program had to be used on a different computer system from the PC, the Apple Macintosh. In this case WordPerfect maintained its market supremacy partly because of its use of the leading hardware. In addition, however, WordPerfect had a system of technical support so wide-ranging and highly developed that it has become an industry legend.

BELOW: *Apple Macintosh data systems director John Crane with a range of his products in 1986. Computer firms may compete with rivals on the basis of price, but many other factors, such as technical superiority, after-sales service, and branding, are also important.*

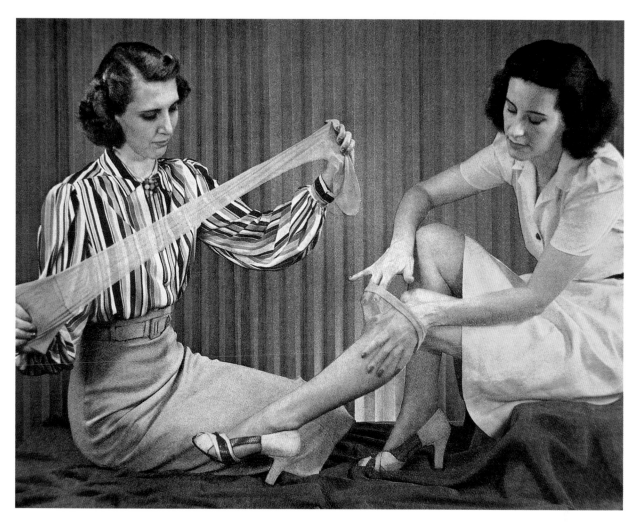

In scientific instrumentation firms also use after-sales services to compete, often organizing training courses for users and hardware and software helplines. Another example of this is with automobiles. In the 20 years from 1980 to 2000, Japanese car manufacturers effectively used after-sales service to increase their share of the U.K. market. By offering a three-year warranty, they took sales away from their western competitors, who, at the time, were offering only 12 months' warranty on new cars.

Branding

The spreadsheet software example described above also illustrates the principle of branding. In perfect competition products must be homogeneous. This means that they are all the same and cannot be differentiated in any way. The spreadsheet software program is a product that could have been homogeneous. If every manufacturer had given the product exactly the same functions and produced it for the same operating system, then there would not have been any difference between different makes. In reality, however, manufacturers vied with each other for increased market share by providing features that were not available on

the spreadsheets provided by competing firms, and they gambled heavily on the future of computing operating systems. The wide choice of spreadsheets that became available allowed consumers to exhibit brand loyalty.

Indeed, the computer industry in general has provided many other examples of the same economic phenomenon. The first computers were completely individual. Almost everything about them was unique. It was impossible to transfer data from one brand of machine to another, and programs were written so as to be specific to a particular brand of machine. Users became locked into using only one producer because they were unwilling to bear the cost of manually entering data again onto an alternative system, even if that system was more technologically advanced. Such a policy restricted innovation. It was consequently hard to sell new and better computers.

Then in 1969 CP/M was introduced. It was the first common operating system across a range of computers that used a common microchip. It soon resulted in a tremendous number of new application products for these machines. The original computer suppliers were operating like monopolists in their own

ABOVE: When the Du Pont Corporation developed nylon stockings in the 1930s, it patented and branded its product to protect its R&D breakthrough.

VHS vs. Betamax: the video recorder

The story of the struggle between the VHS and Betamax video recorder systems is full of significance for economists—it exhibits the principles of ownership and economies of scale; it is a classic example of a case in which an inferior product does not dominate the market because of economies of scale; it is also an example of marketing ingenuity.

The first commercially viable video recorder was introduced in 1956 by the Ampex Corporation. It was tube-operated and intended for the professional market. Attempts by Ampex to reach agreements with other electronics firms to transistorize the machine and market it to home users were a failure. These attempts resulted in a variety of incompatible models, and it was not until 1969 that Sony developed a cartridge-based system for the home market. Sony also attempted to enter into agreements with other electronics firms, looking to create a standard product. Again, the video recorder was not a success in the home market, although Sony had some success in the educational market. Several other attempts were made to produce home-use videos, all without success.

Betamax and VHS
Then in 1975 Sony introduced a model called Betamax, while at the same time JVC was developing a system called VHS (Video Home System). Sony again tried to involve other manufacturers in producing a home-recording standard product, but it was not until 1976 that a meeting took place. The meeting assured the supremacy of Betamax and VHS over other formats.

It was established that the main difference between the two products was that JVC was attempting to achieve a two-

BELOW: The story of the development of the VCR and its cassettes is a revealing case study for economists.

hour recording time against Betamax's single hour. This longer recording time was achieved through the development by JVC of a new tape-threading mechanism and a larger cassette. Other technical differences between Betamax and VHS were quite trivial.

The differences between the two technologies developed as a result of Sony and JVC having different perceptions of consumer requirements. Sony took the view that a small, compact cassette for easy carrying was important to people. JVC and its associates, on the other hand, believed that a more important feature would be to have a long recording capability that would enable the recording from beginning to end of feature films shown on television.

More tape for less money
In 1977 the VHS machines were launched with a four-hour recording capability. A marketing battle ensued between the two corporations, with both cutting prices in an attempt to beat the competition. Still, the technological similarity of the two products made it difficult for one to achieve supremacy over the other. The most significant difference remained the recording time. When Betamax increased its recording time, VHS increased its own even more. Other improvements included maximizing the picture quality by increasing the tape speed, but this was achieved by both firms. Various studies found little picture-quality difference between the two. Despite the similar technologies, VHS was quick to outsell Betamax throughout the world. By 1983 Betamax's share of world demand for video recorders was down to 12 percent. Sony was the only manufacturer not to have adopted the VHS standard by 1985.

Did the market fail?
The story is one of a standards battle. It is one in which most consumers initially switched between the two products but finally settled on a choice based on a feature that they preferred—the longer recording time that was available with VHS. The Betamax video recorder had a minority following. It was easier to use for complex editing and special effects. As a result, it became popular with professional users. This propagated a myth among some that Betamax had higher picture quality. This is, however, not the case, as already stated. In fact, more recent attempts to introduce a super-picture-quality VHS have failed commercially. Consumers are unwilling to pay extra for higher quality, and furthermore, the regular VHS now has a picture quality that is as good as the human eye can detect and better than regular TV transmission signals.

As the battle between the two standards was repeated in many different national markets, all with the same outcome, there is no evidence that consumers' choice was due to insufficient investment by Betamax. Buyers simply preferred a particular standard and were confident that other users would make the same decision. As with the QWERTY keyboard (*see* box, page 63) there has probably not been a lock-in to a lower-standard product. The market has not failed. It can be said that there were two standards battles, even two different products, one of which was required by the consumer and one by the professional.

little markets. Technological change forced them to compete, and the increased competition resulted in a wider range of products and lower prices. According to competition theory, this is the effect that would be expected.

Technology and patents

Patents are a means of protecting an invention from exploitation by other potential manufacturers. The inventor can apply for a patent that prevents anyone else from making the product or profiting from it. Although it will only last for a certain period, it allows inventors to recoup development costs. Patents have traditionally been applicable only to physical processes or machinery. Attempts to patent computer software have failed, and writers of such products gain protection under the copyright acts of various countries. Many examples of patents exist, some of them quite frivolous:
● Patent No. US4429685. A method of growing unicorns. It is claimed to produce unicorns of higher intelligence and physical attributes. Claimed to be useful for producing guard animals. Involves surgical procedures on a one-week old goat.
● Patent No. W09701384. A leash for walking imaginary pets.
● Patent No. FR2694256. An amphibious horse-drawn vehicle.

On a more serious note, patents have been widely used in the pharmaceutical industry, where the research and development costs of drugs are notoriously high. Without the protection of a patent there would be little incentive to invest in such products. Many industrial and chemical processes have also been patented.

Advances in technology and competition
In June 1996 the National Center for Policy Analysis noted that developments in information technology (IT), the computer industry, and the Internet are driving economies nearer to the state of perfect knowledge in which prices, product quality, and availability can be determined everywhere at the same time. Thus e-commerce, as it has become known, is reducing barriers of entry to new firms, so moving certain markets closer to perfect competition.

A good case in point is the growth of Amazon, a bookselling operation that takes customer orders over the Internet. When it set up in 1995, its growth was hampered by the fact that a large section of its potential market did not yet have access to the worldwide web. Then people were still afraid to buy from the firm in case their credit-card details—which had to be entered on the Amazon order form—were intercepted online and used by fraudsters. These difficulties have now largely

been overcome: PCs have proliferated, and there is a trusted security mechanism in place to deter dishonest hackers. Some economists have identified the growth of Amazon—which is now firmly established in the marketplace—as confirmation of the current success and the long-term durability of e-commerce.

The low entry costs in e-commerce are seen as one factor in the creation of a market structure characterized by the concept of perfect competition. Prices become determined by the concept of normal profit. New technology and innovation are seen as the primary source of profit, and the increased interest in online trading in shares may completely change the way in which firms are financed (*see* page 79).

BELOW: The success of the bookseller Amazon.com is indicative of the rapid growth of e-commerce— trade over the Internet.

With growth in Internet use, then, those markets that are using the service move closer to some of the conditions of perfect competition. The size of the web doubles every eight months, and the amount of traffic—the number of times people log on—doubles every 100 days. At the beginning of 2000 it was estimated that 300 million people had access to the Internet worldwide, and in the United States 50 percent of users were e-commerce ready—that is, willing and able to start using the Internet for commercial transactions such as shopping. In 1998 Forrester Research Inc. predicted that by 2003 online retail sales in the United States would be 6 percent of total retail sales in the country. Also important is the predominance of sites written in English; estimates suggest 80 percent of web users speak English.

The growth of firms

As we have seen, firms and businesses face different markets, different levels of competition, and might have quite different goals and ideas about how they would like to progress. In general, however, most firms look to expand their level of operations in order to achieve increased revenues and increased profits. The owners of the firm—whether the proprietor, the partners, or the shareholders—will then become more wealthy. If a firm increases in size, it can take advantage of economies of scale by buying and selling goods and services from and to a larger area, and expanding production overseas markets.

Most firms, particularly smaller firms, choose to expand their operations by reinvesting their profits in the production process. This increased input may finance the purchase of more raw materials or capital goods (more machinery, another vehicle, a new factory, and so on), the employment of a larger workforce, or perhaps greater investment in research and development (R&D) on new products and new production methods (*see* page 28, How a business works).

Capital vs. labor

The four factors of production—land, labor, capital, and entrepreneurship—are all necessary for the production of goods and services, and an increase in one or all of them is necessary for a firm to grow. Because producers normally attempt to maximize profits, in the short run they expand their output to meet an increase in demand by increasing the use of the cheapest factor of production. Traditionally that has been labor. The first stage in expansion therefore might be to increase the hours worked by the existing laborforce in the form

BELOW: Many cars but no people—the advance of automation has enabled factories like this to make massive savings on their wage bills.

Why are U.S. banks so small?

The growth of U.S. banks has been restricted by a deliberate government policy to prevent the development of a monopoly in the banking sector. In *The American Banker* of July 17, 1996, Calvani and Miller explained:

"The relatively small size of U.S. banks is not fortuitous; our state and national legislators have made a conscious decision to impede the emergence of large banking institutions within the United States. The proscription against holding equity positions, interstate banking, the Glass-Steagall Act, state branch banking laws, and so forth, all dictate a particular result. Our banks are small because we have wanted them that way."

ABOVE: *The Union Bank building in downtown Los Angeles, California.*

of overtime. If the increase in demand were seen as more permanent, then extra labor would have to be employed. Eventually, if the increase in demand persisted, more capital would be employed and eventually more land.

In many parts of the world the increasing costs of labor and the falling costs of some capital have, in certain industries, changed this trend. It is often now more cost-effective for firms to employ extra capital and reduce the use of labor. So, for example, in the car industry automation has become the norm. Instead of employing masses of skilled workers, it is now more cost-effective to install machines and robots—usually computerized—and have a small number of workers controlling the system. Another example is packaging. In the pharmaceutical industry during the 1970s most products were still being packed by hand. Rows of unskilled workers would repetitively count tablets into bottles. Everything moved along a conveyor belt, so that the next woman down the line would screw on the cap, and so on. Most systems like this are now mechanized.

The replacement of men and women by machines has created much controversy. Economists have been concerned that there

could be a fall in demand as workers lost their jobs—there is no point increasing output if there is no chance of selling it. Some industries have as an alternative switched to cheaper labor sources. In an attempt to cut costs, industries have been moved to countries where labor is cheap. Southeast Asia has been one of the main areas to benefit from this development. However, some western countries—notably the United States—have been vociferous in their demands for the imposition of international labor standards, claiming that South Korea in particular has a poor record in this area.

Classical economists have opposed international labor standards on the grounds that such regulations interfere with the doctrine of comparative advantage. These economists treat labor as just another input cost. Meddling with this status quo is seen as rendering the international trading system less efficient. Other commentators challenge this view, saying that there is so great a disparity between the wage rates in industrialized nations and those in developing countries that there is no real link between the cost and efficiency of labor in either region.

Hostile takeovers

Many mergers and takeovers take place by mutual consent because both parties stand to benefit from the deal. However, this is not always the case. In a minority of cases the firm being approached does not want to be taken over. It may believe, for example, that the merger would not be in the best interests of its shareholders or staff.

Some notable bids
Examples of hostile takeover bids are:

> **ATT for NCR**
> **GE Capital for Kemper**
> **IBM for Lotus**
> **J&J for Cordis**
> **Norfolk & Southern for Conrail**
> **Hilton for ITT**

The hostile takeover will have an acquiring company and a target company. There may also be a "white knight"—the name given to a company with which the target company would rather be associated. In making a bid for the target company, the acquiring company will carefully review the target's vulnerability and weak points.

Assuming that the target is an incorporated company, state law will dictate certain aspects of a takeover. So, for example, in New York two-thirds of the shareholders of the target firm must vote in favor of the takeover, while in Delaware a simple majority applies unless the company charter provides differently. Many other legal aspects will be considered. Consideration of the antitrust laws must also be made. Once the bid is public, other companies may join in, white knights among them.

Growth by integration

BELOW: American On Line (AOL) chairman Steve Case (left) and Time Warner chairman Gerald Levin announce their merger in January 2000.

As outlined above, another method of obtaining growth is by integration or merger. There are three types of merger: horizontal, vertical, and conglomerate. A horizontal merger takes place between two firms in the same industry at the same stage of production—if Ford and General Motors were to amalgamate, for example, that would be a horizontal merger. A vertical merger occurs between two firms at different stages of production in the same industry. There are two types of vertical merger: forward integration, in which a supplier merges with one of its buyers, as for example when an automobile manufacturer buys a sales dealership; and backward integration, in which a purchaser buys one of its suppliers—e.g., if a newspaper buys a paper mill. Oil companies often exhibit a high degree of vertical integration, owning, for example, oilfields, tankers for transport, oil refineries, and gas stations.

Finally, a conglomerate merger is the amalgamation of two companies with no common interest or apparent synergy. All mergers are undertaken in order to secure sources of supply or markets. Integration is an important means by which smaller firms can become much larger firms quite quickly. Among other things, larger firms can finance high-cost research-and-development programs more easily than smaller ones.

Integration in the computer industry

The computer industry is a prime example of one in which integration was important in some areas. At the end of World War II in 1945 the computer industry worldwide was still in its infancy. Most major developments had taken place at the University of Pennsylvania in the United States and the universities of Cambridge and Manchester in the United Kingdom. High technology tends to develop around universities.

By the 1960s expansion in computers had continued in the United States and the United Kingdom, but was now also taking place in Japan. The differing ways in which computer firms grew and integrated in these countries was (and is) partly due to different government attitudes and levels of intervention. These different attitudes resulted in the development of a range of vastly different customer bases.

The original computers were developed almost entirely for military use. In the United States there was immediate recognition of the potential of the growing commercial data-processing market. Japan, on the other hand, had been devastated during World War II and in the years after 1945 rejected military ventures of any kind. From the 1960s, however, the Japanese rapidly acquired information technology expertise and competed with the United State for commercial markets. During this period, although British IT firms lost ground in world commercial markets to the United States and Japan, they kept themselves going by supplying U.K. government defense contracts.

The computer industry is highly dependent on the need for continuous, costly research and development (R&D). In Japan vertical integration was the means by which firms achieved the size necessary to fund this R&D.

Many Japanese computer companies carried out all stages in the production process: they made their own components, assembled the machines, and marketed them.

In the United States, by contrast, the only vertically integrated computer firm was IBM. Other producers specialized in one stage of production only. In the United States this type of market organization was made possible by the rapid and early domination of the world data-processing industry. The nature of this market meant that firms were required to offer specialized services to their customers.

In the United Kingdom the continued success of the computer industry depended on government defense contracts. They were often large, needed long-term financing, and could involve considerable research. The most successful companies in obtaining U.K. government contracts were integrated companies such as Racal and Ferranti.

Integration and merger

The term integration is used to describe a particular concept of mergers. It is the process of producing a larger organization by the merger of two or more firms. The number of mergers in the United States and throughout the world is increasing. As reported in the Statement of

ABOVE: The British Army officer commanding this air defense unit is wearing a helmet sighting system made by Ferranti, one of the main firms to benefit from continued U.K. government military spending.

The Herfindahl-Hirschman Index

In 1982 antitrust organizations began using the Herfindahl-Hirschman Index (HHI), rather than the concentration ratio, to measure concentration. The index adds up the squares of market shares, normally mulitiplying this figure by 10,000. Consider an industry with 4 firms, each having an equal market share:

HHI	=	0.25 squared + 0.25 squared + 0.25 squared +0.25 squared
	=	0.0625 + 0.0625 + 0.0625 + 0.0625 = 0.25
	=	0.25 x 10,000 = 2,500

The concentration ratio for a 4-firm industry, on the other hand, would be worked out as follows:

CR4	=	0.25 + 0.25 + 0.25 + 0.25 = 1

Now suppose the first two firms merge, and firms three and four also merge. The new values are:

HHI	=	0.5 squared + 0.5 squared = 0.25 + 0.25 = 0.5
	=	0.5 x 10,000 = 5,000

CR4	=	0.5 + 0.5 = 1

The HHI has changed, but the CR4 has not.

Broadly speaking:

An HHI of < 1,000 is unconcentrated
An HHI of between 1,000 and 1,800 is moderately concentrated
An HHI above 1,800 is highly concentrated

(In practice HHI is based on calculations for the 6 largest firms in the industry)

the Federal Trade Commission on June 16, 1998, in Washington, D.C., the cases reported to the antitrust agencies under the Hart-Scott-Rodino Act have increased from 1,529 in the 1991 fiscal year to an estimated 4,500 in 1998.

In the view of Professor Pitofsky of the Federal Trade Commission the nature and motives of merger activity have changed. During the 1980s many mergers were "junk bond" fueled. They involved unrelated businesses that were targeted by the raiders to generate cash. Parts of firms were sold off and whole firms destroyed as a productive unit. One consequence of this was an increased level of unemployment as workers lost their jobs. Today's mergers are more likely to be motivated by developments in a rapidly changing economy. Professor Pitofsky identifies the following possible motives:

● Globalization of competition. For most products, as well as for many services, markets are becoming worldwide. As a result, the benefits of a merger might include an improved international distribution system, improved knowledge of local markets, the ability to take advantage of economies of scale, and complementary products. Complementary goods are goods for which consumption is interdependent—for example, compact discs and compact disc players, and cars and gas.

● Deregulation. In recent years mergers have been favored in areas where deregulation is anticipated—that is, where a lifting or reduction of control by government is expected to take place in an industry. Such changes are taking place in the United States in the electricity industry, telecommunications, and banking. Deregulation often induces greater competition and encourages market entry across traditional industry lines. So, for example, in the case of banking banks now provide a wider range of financial services than ever before—it is now the norm for them to offer insurance and pension plans in addition to their traditional services.

● Industry downsizing and consolidation. They were more important in the 1980s and early 1990s, but are still of significance to the defense industries. Many suppliers in this industry now face lower order levels and fewer projects. They tend to pare their operations to the minimum sustainable level (rationalize) and thereby reduce administration costs.

● Technological change. Mergers can enable a firm to acquire technological know-how. That has been particularly true in the cases of the communications and pharmaceutical industries.

● Strategic mergers. Some mergers involve a firm merging with a direct competitor, perhaps in order to eliminate competition and boost its market share. This type of merger can most easily result in the new organization having market dominance and can encourage collusion because of increased concentration. Some therefore believe these mergers should be given antitrust attention.

● Financial market considerations. During the late 1990s low interest rates and inflation encouraged investment in the United States. That was reflected in a booming stock market. As a result, more and more mergers became financed by exchanges of stock rather than by the transfer of cash (*see* box, page 79).

Concentration ratios

Economists have defined various types of market. At one end of the competition scale is perfect competition, and at the other is monopoly. In between, various states of competition are recognized, for example, oligopoly and monopolistic competition.

Until 1982 the degree of competition in a market was measured by concentration ratios. The ratio was determined by adding together the market shares of the three, four, or five largest firms in an industry to see if there was an oligopoly or a monopoly. The Herfindahl-Hirschman Index has been seen as a more accurate measure since then (*see* box opposite).

A major reason for the variations in concentration ratios between industries is the different level of output at which economies of scale start to be exhausted. Current information about concentration ratios in U.S. industries can be obtained on CD-ROM from the U.S. Census Bureau or at the website <<http:// www.census.gov/mp/www/pub/mfg/msmfg04f.html >>.

According to economic theorists, in general, the more concentrated an industry, the less competitive it will be, while the greater the number of firms in an industry, the more competitive that industry will be. The more competitive an industry is, the less likely it is to act against the public interest. This principle is illustrated in the quotation in the box on page 71, Why are U.S. banks so small?.

Growth and network markets

As we have seen, firms want to grow for a variety of reasons. An important area of growth now recognized in economics affects network markets. Network markets increase in value as the number of people in the market increases. Therefore network industries will want to expand in order to become more attractive to potential customers. One example of a network effect is the telephone: as the number of people with a phone increases, it becomes more valuable. The same can be said for many communications products, such as faxes.

Network markets differ from others in that the benefits of increased size come from the demand side—the greater the network, the higher the price that consumers are willing to pay—rather than from the supply side, in which the costs of production are reduced as a result of increased size. This increase in value comes about because the members of the network are connected to each other. The connection can be literal, as in the case of the telephone or the fax. Alternatively, it can be notional, as in the case of the members of a trade union. The connection implies some continuing interaction in the future.

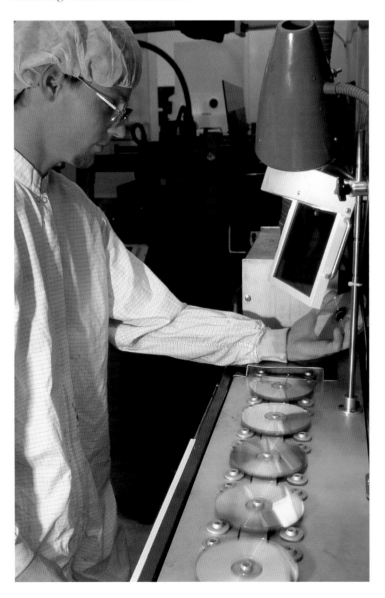

BELOW: A firm may benefit from merging with a company producing a complementary product.Compact discs (CDs) and CD players are complementary products—consumers are unlikely to have one without the other.

Another feature of network markets is that they are owned. The concept of ownership varies from the absolute ownership that exists when a network has some physical connecting media, such as telephone lines, to a less explicit notion of ownership, as in the trade union. In this case the network is owned by the members and becomes more valuable as its membership grows. The larger the union, the greater its negotiating power, and the more it can do for its members. This contrasts with economies of scale in production, which are available to any firm that grows in size.

BELOW: The telephone system is an example of an economic network market.

Financing growth

Growth is an objective of all sectors of the economy and a government objective for the economy as a whole. An increase in the aggregate level of output is measured by changes in gross domestic product (GDP). Government must perform a balancing act, encouraging growth and at the same time keeping inflation—the rate of which tends to increase when an economy is expanding rapidly—under control. Consumers want to see their incomes grow so that they can purchase more goods and services, and have a better standard of living. Similarly, firms will want to grow. To do so, they will invariably need to increase the quantity of land, labor, entrepreneurship, and capital that they use. Assuming that firms are using their current factors of production to full capacity, growth will necessitate the acquisition of more.

In the long run all factors of production are variable. In the short run, at least one will be fixed. Increasing the usage of all factors involves increasing the scale of output. It is important to remember that money itself is not a resource. It represents a claim on resources, and any firm wishing to grow must be able to raise the extra money that is required to purchase the required factors.

Financing from retained profits

By far the cheapest source of such funds will be the firm's own retained profits. Note that the existence of such a source implies the presence of supernormal or abnormal profits. Normal profits will be distributed to the owners of the business in the form of dividends to shareholders, for example. In the long run this means that the firm must have some monopoly power if it is going to fund expansion through reinvesting its profits. This is because if it existed in conditions of perfect competition, there would only be normal profits. A conventional firm will try to grow so as to take advantages of economies of scale. Retained profits are limited, and they will be reduced by taxation.

Bank loans

Another possible source of funds is a bank loan. Firms borrow from banks mainly to overcome short-term cash-flow problems. The bank provides them with an overdraft service, after which it is agreed and expected that the firm's current balance will go in and out of debt. However, longer-term borrowing from banks may have serious disadvantages. Financing expansion from such sources will not only result in the payment of high rates of interest but may also result in the bank wanting its own representatives on the board, so

that it has some say in how the business is run. This will particularly be the case if the loans are large or the proposed expansion is risky.

Venture capital

One very important development for firms is the increased availability of venture capital. It is a high-risk, high-return investment in support of business creation and growth. A venture-capital firm will raise large sums—sometimes as much as $50 million—to invest in the development and growth of other firms. The legal structure of such a fund is a limited partnership. Those who invest money in the fund are known as the limited partners (LPs). Those who invest the funds in developing companies are known as general partners (GPs). Generally, LPs contribute 99 percent of the committed capital and GPs 1 percent.

Venture-capital firms receive payment for their services in two ways. First, they receive an annual management fee. It is usually about 2.5 percent of the money they invest. In addition they receive income from the allocation of the net income of the fund. It is usually obtained from the sale or distribution of the stock of the companies in which they invest.

A venture-capital fund usually has a life of no more than about 10 years. The first stage is fundraising, which typically takes between six months and a year. Sources of investment are state and corporate pension funds, public and private endowments, and personal investors. The second stage—which lasts between three and six years—comprises the sourcing and investment of the funds. Sourcing refers to the process by which the venture-capital outfit finds the firms that are in need of investment. In the third stage, which lasts until the closure of the fund, the companies in which the venture capitalists have invested are helped to grow. The venture-capital outfit will own equity (stocks or shares) in the firm and will have a representative on the its board of executives. The fourth and final stage involves the sale of the firm's stock as the venture capitalists cash in on (liquidate) their investment.

Venture-capital firms judge the worthiness of their potential investments on the basis of four fundamental criteria:
● A strong management team with a proven track record is required.
● The firm should be in a rapidly growing market with good potential. If the firm is

ABOVE: Federal Express is one of many famous U.S. firms that has used venture capital to fund expansion.

ABOVE: *The growth of NASDAQ (National Association of Securities Dealers Automated Quotations) has helped the rapid growth of financial investment over the Internet.*

project; but as a rule, the later the stage, the less risk that is involved. In startup companies a return is expected within five to seven years, while established companies are expected to produce a return in two to four years.

The final step for a company is to go public. It is at this point that the venture-capital firm can make a large profit by selling. If a venture-capital firm had obtained a 40 percent stake in a company by giving loans of $6 million, and a market valuation of $150 million is achieved, then its investment becomes worth $60 million. Among the many well-known firms that have received venture-capital assistance are Apple, Microsoft, Novell, and Federal Express. They are all examples of what are known in the industry as "home-run" deals. Home-run deals refer to investments on which there is a return of between 20 and 100 times or even more on the original sum advanced.

Issuing shares

Firms with a limited liability status raise their initial funds by the issue of stocks (shares). The ownership of these shares denotes ownership of the business; and when a firm is public, these stocks can be bought and sold on the stock market. When a firm originally issues a share, it will have an issue price. For example, if a firm wishes to raise $50,000 dollars, then it could issue 5,000 shares at $10 each. Once the shares are on the market, they acquire a market value. It could be less or more than the issue price. Over time the share price will change according to how well the firm is perceived to be performing.

The stock market has two component parts. The primary market is for new stocks that are being issued by companies to raise finance. Payment for these shares goes to the company and is used to purchase raw materials, capital stock, to pay new employees, and so on. The secondary market is for shares that have already been issued and are owned by investors. The payment for these simply causes the stocks to change ownership, and the seller receives the cash. The firm does not receive anything in this case. All that has happened is that ownership of part of the firm has changed hands.

The existence of a secondary market is necessary if the primary market is to be successful. Without the secondary market investors could never get their money back. The size of this secondary market is growing, and many parts of it have received an added boost from the Internet. At the end of 1998 American households owned $8.8 trillion in stocks and shares, often through mutual funds that make large-scale investments with the smaller contributions of many individuals. This is four times what was owned in 1990 and

operating in competition, the market must be able to support at least two firms. The firm's distribution channels must be well established.
● There should be few technical risks as regards the firm's product, and it should be well differentiated from competitors' products. The product should have a good profit margin and have an opportunity for repeat sales. It should not be the only product of the firm.
● Assessment is also made of the exit costs from the industry. Sunk capital—investments that cannot be recovered, such as, for example, the money lost through depreciation— should be kept to a minimum.

Venture-capital firms usually specialize in a particular type of industry. Popular areas include biotechnology, computer software, communications, and retail. They will also specialize in one particular stage of financing. Some may specialize in financing the start of a

Using stock as currency

Some firms use their stock to finance expansion—when they buy other companies, they pay for the shares not with cash but with shares in their own firm. One advantage of this is that it enables the sellers to put off paying tax on the deals they have made.

The Cintas Corporation of Cincinnati is a prime example of a firm that has used its stock as a currency to expand. In 1973 its sales revenues were $1 million. Then its value increased 5 times in 5 years. By the end of 1999 its sales revenues were $1.2 billion, and its stock was worth more than $7 billion. Between 1984 and 1998 Cintas used stock worth $716 million to acquire 157 companies. In 1998 alone Cintas made 48 acquisitions worth $361 million.

In buying other firms using stock instead of cash, U.S. firms in general are also able to combine operations. However, amalgamations often lead to job losses—210,521 U.S. jobs were lost in this way in three months in 1998.

equivalent to a year's GDP in the United States. The individuals who own these shares include many who are using the Internet to buy. They frequently have no expertise in investment matters and do not seek the advice of professionals who do. A matter of concern is that this new breed of investor knows only an upbeat, buoyant economy (a bull market) and has yet to meet a bear market—that is, one in which prices are in general decline. The

BELOW: This statue on Wall Street was erected to commemorate the bull market that was brought to an end by the stock market crash of 1987.

Dow Jones Index, which measures the value of shares, indicates that $1,000 invested at the end of 1993 would now be worth:

$2,760 on average across all shares
$2,900 if invested in Standard & Poor's stocks
$3,340 if invested in NASDAQ Composite index stocks.

Between 1965 and 1990 the number of Americans owning stock doubled from 10 percent to 20 percent of the population. By 1997 it had more than doubled again to 43 percent. The rising market means that businesses are able to find more money for expansion and growth. From 1995 to 2000 firms raised $183 billion in initial public offerings (IPOs).

For much of the 1960s and 1970s inflation was high, and investors preferred to own assets, such as real estate, rather than shares. As wages rose, the real cost of paying off debt fell, encouraging people to take out loans. Many Americans became risk-takers. A survey by the Opinion Research Corporation in 1998 found that investors expected to earn 17.4 percent a year on stocks over the next 10 years. The actual rate for the previous decade was only 9 percent. The younger the investor and the lower the income, the greater the expectations. For such people the growth of U.S. business was a tempting chance to get rich quick.

ABOVE: Updates on the New York Dow Jones Index are tracked all over the world—here the price is displayed in San Francisco, California.

SEE ALSO

• Volume 1, page 6: The stock market

• Volume 3, page 43: Government and business

• Volume 3, page 105: Organizations and boards

• Volume 5, page 14: Competition and perfect competition

• Volume 5, page 51: Intellectual property

• Volume 5, page 77: Nonprice competition

• Volume 5, page 109: Technology

How firms behave in the real world

In the study of economics theoretical examples are drawn from an idealized world in which outside influences are constant and thus do not have to be considered. In the real world, however, firms have to react decisively to rapidly changing external factors.

Firms are organizations that produce goods—such as automobiles, computers, and processed foods—and services—such as banking and telecommunications. They use resources known as the factors of production—land, labor, capital, and entrepreneurship—to produce these commodities. While firms are usually involved in the process of production in order to maximize their profits, economic theory asserts that the pursuit of this goal will at the same time satisfy the wants of consumers.

This theory is founded on a series of strict conditions and assumptions—that is, the assumptions of perfect competition (see below). In reality, however, these conditions are seldom met. In this chapter we look at some of the strategies and problems of firms in the real world. Most firms and corporations are looking to expand production and increase their profits. The pursuit of these goals will often involve businesses taking advantage of the fact that they do not operate in perfectly competitive markets.

Perfect competition vs monopoly

The study of economics attempts to explain how society solves the problem of using scarce resources to satisfy the needs of everyone in that society and the rest of the world. Many theories have been put forward, some of which all economists agree on, while others remain the subject of fierce debate.

Theories to predict behavior

Most economic concepts use theoretical examples or models of the real economy—the model for perfect competition and the model for monopoly, for example. In the interests of accuracy these models must be simple enough to allow the theory to be formulated while at the same time being as close to reality as possible.

Theories of the behavior of firms have traditionally been concerned with only two variables—the price of output (production) and the quantity of output per unit of time. The latter is a measurement of how many goods can be produced in, for example, one day or one hour. From these theories further

BELOW: Firms within a firm—the shops and cafes in this mall are businesses, and the building itself is operated by another firm. Most people in the western world deal with business almost every day.

attempts have been made to determine how much a firm should produce and what its motives for production are.

The theories state that the only reason for the output having a price is that the resources used by the firms (the factors of production) are scarce—they are said to have an opportunity cost. In deciding to use resources for one purpose, society cannot then put them to another use. If there were sufficient resources to produce everything people need, output would not command a price.

In the real world firms are of different types and sizes. Many firms are owned by a single proprietor, others by stockholders (shareholders). Together with their customers, who are known as consumers, firms operate in a market or markets. The market can be either a physical place—such as a shopping mall—or an abstract concept—such as the market for petroleum. In this marketplace firms compete to supply their product to consumers. Different types of competition exist, and economists have found it convenient to define two extreme situations. These two markets can be thought of as being at opposite ends of a spectrum. At one end is perfect competition (as mentioned above), and at the other is monopoly. In between the two are various forms of imperfect competition; most firms operating in the real world actually face imperfectly competitive markets.

Perfect competition

The following are the five main conditions that must prevail to enable a market to exhibit perfect competition:

● There must be a large number of buyers and

The U.S. federal antitrust laws

The Sherman Act—originated in 1890—is the principal law committing the United States to a free-market economy. Congress treated this law very seriously, and there was only one dissenting vote. It outlaws all contracts and conspiracies that unreasonably restrain interstate trade. It also makes it unlawful to monopolize any part of interstate trade. It intervenes only when the growth in the level of market share is being obtained by anticompetitive practices. Violations of the act are criminal felonies. Individual violators can be fined up to $350,000 and sentenced to up to three years in a federal prison. Corporations can be fined up to $10 million.

The Clayton Act is an example of civil law. It carries no criminal penalties. First passed in 1914, it was significantly amended in 1950. It prohibits mergers or acquisitions (takeovers) that might lessen competition. If economic analysis shows a likely increase in consumer prices for a product, the government will challenge any relevant mergers. Mergers above a certain size must be notified to the Antitrust Division and the Federal Trade Commission. The Federal Trade Commission Act is also a civil act. This legislation created the Federal Trade Commission (FTC) and prohibits methods of unfair competition in interstate commerce.

sellers (i.e., consumers and producers), none of whom is individually big enough to influence the price of the product.

● Each firm must produce a homogeneous good—that is, the products from all suppliers should be perceived to be absolutely identical to one another.

● There should be complete resource mobility. It must be possible to move land, labor, entrepreneurship, and capital freely within and between different uses and markets.

● Buyers and sellers must have perfect knowledge of the market. This means that all buyers and sellers are aware of the quantities of goods available from every supplier, together with their price, and the quantities of goods required by consumers at whatever price.

● There must be no barriers to entering, or costs of leaving, the market.

For an industry to be categorized as perfectly competitive, all five of the above conditions must be met. If any of the conditions is not met, the industry is not perfectly competitive, and the allocation of resources that results will not be economically efficient.

Economists argue about whether perfect competition exists in the real world. An example of a market that almost fits the picture is that for a firm's shares—a share is defined as a part of the capital of a firm that is offered for sale. If a firm has its shares floated on the stock exchange, the market will consist of the sellers of that one firm's shares and the potential buyers. Now that sellers have access to modern information technology, it can be argued that the market exhibits near-perfect knowledge. Nonetheless, in the real world very few, if any, markets comply with such

LEFT: A satirical U.S. cartoon in which monopoly is depicted as a hungry octopus clasping everything around it in its tentacles before eating it.

strict conditions. As a consequence of these real-life imperfections, firms often have very different strategies and behave very differently from the ways predicted by theories of perfect competition.

Monopoly

A monopoly is said to exist when there is only one firm supplying a particular good or service. The concept is largely theoretical—in the real world there are very few markets that have only one supplier. Legal definitions of monopoly may vary from country to country and over time. In the United States, for example, Section 2 of the Sherman Act (1890) states that monopoly in itself is not illegal but that the monopolization of trade is. For a monopoly to occur there must be:

● The power either to fix prices or to exclude all competition.
● A deliberate attempt to preserve or acquire such power.

In the landmark legal case of the United States vs The Aluminum Company of America (Alcoa) 184 F 2d 416 in 1945, the judge ruled that if one firm controlled 90 percent of the supply of a commodity, that was sufficient to constitute a monopoly; 60 to 64 percent of supply was doubtful, and 33 percent was clearly not enough for a firm to be deemed to have monopoly power.

In the United Kingdom a monopoly is held to exist either when a single firm has at least 25 percent of the market—this is known as a scale monopoly—or when more than one firm has at least 25 percent of the market, and these firms conduct their affairs in such a way as to distort competition—this is known as a complex monopoly.

Antitrust legislation

Economic theory suggests that monopoly can act against the interests of consumers since monopoly companies are at liberty to charge high prices and make excessive profits on their output. Most advanced economies have developed legislation designed to limit or control the growth of monopolies, which are generally agreed to be undesirable.

In the United States the first antitrust legislation was passed in the late 19th century. At the federal level the Antitrust Division of the U.S. Department of Justice has the responsibility of prosecuting under these acts. Individual states also have their own antitrust laws. The historic goal of the antitrust laws was to protect economic freedom and opportunity in the U.S. by promoting competition in the marketplace. There are three major U.S. federal laws governing antitrust—the Sherman Act, the Clayton Act and the Federal Trade Commission Act (*see* box, above left).

Monopolies in the United Kingdom

The approach taken to monopoly, mergers, and so on varies from country to country. In the United Kingdom, for example, since 1948 antimonopoly legislation has been the responsibility of the Monopolies and Mergers Commission. However, while the U.S. Department of Justice has the power to prosecute offending firms, the Monopolies and Mergers Commission usually acts in an advisory capacity to government ministers, since it merely refers to various acts of parliament to advise government ministers on the best course of action to be taken in a particular set of circumstances. The commission has frequently been criticized for accepting firms' assurances that they are not operating a monopoly and for habitually tending toward the benign view that company mergers—when two or more firms combine to make a single, larger whole—tend to operate in the public interest.

How firms grow and compete

Depending on the market conditions they face, firms will adopt different strategies to expand their market share—the amount of total output they produce in the industry compared to other firms—and to compete with other firms in the industry. Naturally, a firm

BELOW: Penguin Books— originally an independent British publisher of cheap paperback books— eventually became a part of The Pearson Group, a vast multinational corporation.

ABOVE: Internet-wired tables at the @ Cafe in the East Village, New York City.

will be more competitive if it can reduce its costs. If it faces lower costs than other firms producing the same product, it can either make a larger profit, or it can reduce its prices and claim a greater share of the market. Whether or not the firm can maintain these high profits or its larger market share depends on how easy it is for other firms to enter the market. We will look at this in greater detail below.

Economies of scale

A firm may reduce its costs and compete more effectively against other firms if it is able to take advantage of economies of scale. Economies of scale result in the unit cost of production falling as the level of output increases; they are therefore vital in mass production. For example, when manufacturing an automobile, there is a large initial fixed cost in setting up the machinery in the factory; however, once the machinery is running smoothly, the cost of manufacturing each automobile tends to remain constant. From that point on, the more automobiles that can be produced in such a factory, the greater the profit to the manufacturer.

The information technology (IT) industry that developed after the end of World War II in the United States, the United Kingdom, and later in Japan produced enormous changes in industry. In particular, IT has facilitated greater economies of scale in production. To continue the example of the automotive industry, IT has provided firms with advanced robots on the production line. IT has also provided dramatic technological advances that have made computers themselves more widely available and cheaper than ever before.

The following are some of the other ways in which a modern firm can achieve economies of scale and compete more effectively in the marketplace:

Specialization and division of labor

As the scale of production increases, a firm's workers will tend to take on smaller, more repetitive tasks and become more expert at their particular job. Consequently, it becomes possible for the firm to employ a greater number of specialists in various technical areas, and there is more opportunity to introduce new capital.

Indivisibilities

Indivisibilities refer to machinery or plant that may be used to produce a certain level of output. Trying to produce lower levels of output—as might happen, for example, during periods when sales are poor, and there is

The failure of the dollar coin

ABOVE: The dollar coin was unsuccessful when it was first introduced in the United States partly because it lacked a network (see main text below): no one wanted to use it until they were confident that others were using it, too.

A striking example of network economics is the failure of the dollar coin. Both the United States and Canada have attempted to introduce the dollar coin. What became known as the Susan B. Anthony $1 coin in the United States was popularly judged to be a failure because of its poor design, which made it look too much like the quarter.

The problem may be explained in terms of network economics by reference to vending machines. The $1 coin can make higher-value transactions in vending machines easier, but only if the vending machine owners pay for the conversion of machines to accept the coins. They will do so only if the public is seen to use the coins. Likewise, the public will use them only if they see them as widely accepted. Neither of these expectations was met. A similar problem arose in Canada despite a more intensive government campaign, which included withdrawal of the paper dollar bill. In time, however, the dollar coin was accepted. In the United Kingdom a pound coin was introduced with some resistance at first, with Scotland retaining its own pound note.

---

a surplus of stock—incurs the same production cost as full output. It should also be noted that as a general rule larger, faster machinery is usually more efficient in manufacturing than smaller, slower machinery.

The container principle

Economies of scale may be improved when storage areas such as warehouses can be designed to store the maximum amount of goods. According to the container principle, warehouses can store more than double the quantity if their dimensions are doubled.

By-products

Large-scale production can result in uses being found for the waste materials thereby generated. If they can be made profitable, they are clearly in the economic interests of the firm.

Multistage production

One large factory can take a product through many stages of production, thereby saving on transportation costs.

Spreading overheads

Certain fixed costs (see above) and the provision of new premises such as research laboratories can be spread over a larger output in order to make the firm more profitable.

Financial economies

Large firms are usually able to obtain bank loans at lower rates of interest than small firms because they are considered to be a lower risk.

Bulk buying

A firm may reduce its production costs through the large-scale purchase of raw materials at discount prices.

Network economics

Certain industries depend on, and take advantage of, networks to expand their business operations. Networks are key parts of any production and consumption process, and they provide significant economies of scale. Examples of networks include transportation, communications, and payment systems.

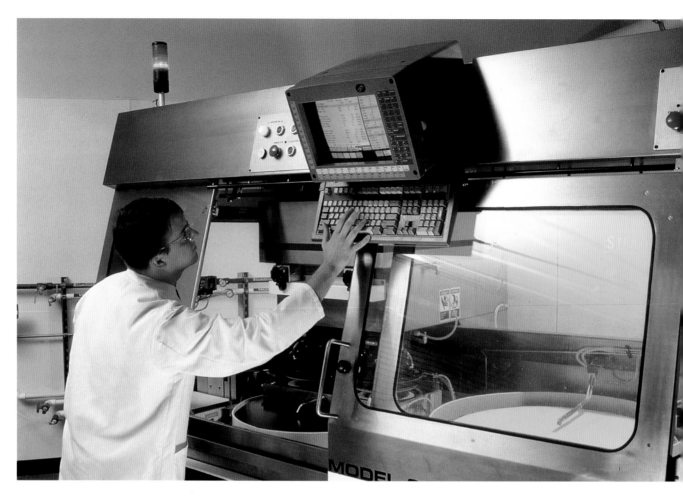

ABOVE: The continued growth and success of business depend to a large extent on firms' ability to attract talent away from the universities and into industry. This is particularly true of scientists.

Networks have two characteristics. The degree of satisfaction—known as utility—an individual gets from a network increases as more people join it, and the techniques of production depend on the methods used by the other firms in the network.

A well-known example of a network is a telephone system. The more people who subscribe to the system, the more useful it will be to all its users. Producers have to make telephones compatible with the overall system and introduce new accessories. This is an economy of scale.

A network can be regarded as a series of nodes connected by various links. Railroads or highways consist of tracks or roads (the links) that connect a series of destinations (the nodes). There are many other examples of networks: oil and gas pipelines, water systems, and computerized airline reservation systems. Examples of network goods include payment checks, point-of-sale systems, and bank debit cards. The nodes here are banks, merchants, and consumers.

In some circumstances networks can be a constraint on business development and have also produced political controversy. The convenience of the automobile has stimulated the growth of road systems in all advanced

economies. The efficient distribution of goods to retail outlets—stores—is an essential feature of any such economy, and roads are used for this distribution. In large cities, however, highways may be occupied by growing numbers of private automobiles, eventually producing traffic gridlock. This is an example of a network getting completely blocked through overuse. One possible solution to this problem is to make greater use of existing rail systems for the distribution of goods, but many argue that to do this would be slower and less efficient, since goods do not get delivered directly to the outlet.

Privatizing networks

In many countries the rail system is or has been government owned, which many believe is more efficient because it is a centrally controled network. Opponents of state-owned industries and networks believe that the railroad system can become more competitive and efficient if it is privatized (privately owned, that is, owned by companies rather than by governments). Other steps toward privatizing transportation networks have included the deregulation in the United Kingdom of bus services—i.e., the removal of preexisting rules and regulations in order to

Downsizing

Some economists believe that in the 1950s and 1960s many companies employed too large a workforce. Economies were demand driven—strong consumer demand resulting in higher prices and scarcities of goods—and in many countries trade unions resisted changes in working practices designed to reduce production costs. Then, in the 1970s and '80s came increased efforts to reduce employers' costs.

One such technique was to reduce workforces by downsizing. Downsizing is a deliberate attempt to reduce the number of employees by staff layoffs, attrition (natural shrinkage—i.e., not replacing workers who leave), and early retirement.

Downsizing is inevitably linked to business decline, since it is often done by firms that are doing badly and can no longer afford to employ as many workers. Downsizing also takes place when firms merge, since tasks in the workplace are now duplicated,

and so surplus workers can be laid off. Its benefits are cited as lower overheads (costs of buildings, space, facilities, electricity, and so on), production cost reduction, reduced bureaucracy, and faster decision making.

A survey of 1,000 U.S. companies by H.F. Stein in 1996 showed that only 22 percent of them achieved their intended improvements in productivity (output per worker) through downsizing, while 15 percent achieved a reduction in bureaucracy. And fewer than 25 percent achieved an increase in payments to shareholders (people with shares in the company). Downsizing is a controversial management technique, often leaving the remaining workers disaffected, insecure, and hostile. Its effects on communities and society as a whole cannot be underestimated. Also, the remaining workers often find that they cannot perform new jobs, and so the company has to recruit additional staff.

---

enable more competition—and the movement of more facilities into the private sector.

The most recent, and arguably the most revolutionary, example of a network is the Internet. As a global network of computers that can communicate directly with each other, the Internet has vast potential for companies to reach new markets and is providing new opportunities for trading. Many suppliers are now offering goods and services through Internet pages.

However, as with many modern technological developments, fresh opportunities have created a whole new range of problems. One of the most serious of them is the security of payment systems on the Internet. Credit-card numbers entered on the Internet have been accessed by criminals who make fraudulent transactions using the information they have stolen. Sophisticated coding techniques and electronic signatures for authorizing commercial and legal documents have now been developed to overcome this problem, but fear about a lack of security remains the biggest brake on the development of the Internet for commerce.

The need for privacy

The rapid growth of the Internet and computerized worldwide communication systems has highlighted the importance of privacy in a thriving world economy. To help guarantee it, most countries have now introduced data-protection legislation. Nevertheless, there have been fundamental disagreements between the United States and the European Union (EU) over the questions of exactly what constitutes privacy and how it should best be protected. Millions of dollars of trade revenue

are at stake until the matter is resolved to the satisfaction of all parties, and consumers can be confident they will not be robbed.

BELOW: Trade unions are important where the interests of a firm differ from those of its workers.

Resource constraints on business growth

While in conditions of perfect competition there should be complete resource mobility—i.e., it should be possible for land, labor, capital, and entrepreneurship to move freely between markets—this is often not the case in the real world. In many markets availability and mobility of factors of production are important constraints on a firm's capacity to expand its operations and take advantage of economies of scale and networks.

Immobility of labor

The development of computing and IT has resulted in a classic case of immobility of labor (labor being the key factor of production). Labor is defined by economists as human effort that can be either physical or mental. Intellectual labor was needed immediately after World War II, when the IT industry, in its early stages of development, depended on centers of expertise. They were located chiefly at the University of Pennsylvania in the United States and at the universities of Cambridge and Manchester in the United Kingdom.

Academics, working in these universities and at other centers of excellence, were difficult to entice away to commercial establishments in different geographical locations. They not only wanted high salaries but also needed to be part of an organization that had international recognition. Thus additional technical staff had to be trained, and this took time. Labor can be immobile for other reasons, too. Workers want to stay with their families and friends, and a move to another area can involve extra cost and problems in finding new housing and schools for their children. Workforces do not undertake geographical upheavals lightly.

As new industries develop, it is often found that workers' skills do not match the new job requirements. A classic example is the rapid growth of new technology in the workplace, requiring new IT skills in many different trades. This mismatch of skills is a structural problem that can be solved only through retraining programs. Governments throughout the world have also attempted to make labor more mobile. One common means of achieving this is by trying to make the workforce better trained and more flexible in its attitude to working practices.

Immobility of capital

Land and capital—two of the other factors of production—can also be highly immobile between markets. In economics the term "land" is taken to include natural resources, such as minerals, timber, and water, while "capital" encompasses human-made resources such as machinery, factories, and stock. Money gives people the power to purchase these resources.

If a firm faced perfect competition, land and capital would both be available instantly at market-driven prices, and no single user,

BELOW: In a supermarket shoppers may have to choose between several different brands of the same product. If there are no significant price differences, their decision may be influenced by brand loyalty.

would be able to dominate or influence the market for these resources. In real markets, however, this is seldom, if ever, the case, since various different groups have a degree of economic power—large employers, labor unions, landlords, and large owners of capital are able to influence the market to their own advantage. In so doing, they are able to achieve a greater share of the national income.

Imperfect competition

The ability of some groups to influence markets means that most are imperfect. They are said to be existing under conditions of imperfect competition. The two most important examples of this type are monopolistic competition and oligopoly.

Monopolistic competition

The American economist Edward Chamberlin (1899-1967) first described monopolistic competition in the 1930s. Each firm in this type of market has some power in that it is able to decide what price to charge for its products. Unlike a monopoly situation, however, monopolistic competition requires a large number of firms. Each firm has a small share of the total market and will have a minimal effect on other firms. It therefore does not have to worry about how its rivals will react. This condition is known as independence.

For monopolistic competition to exist there has to be freedom of entry into the market; any firm wishing to set up business must be able to do so. So, for example, a company could open a store selling the same goods as another previously established firm down the street.

Products in a monopolistic market are heterogeneous—that is, firms produce their own product, which is different from that produced by other firms. This phenomenon is known as product differentiation. Differentiated products include items such as automobiles, computers, and soft drinks, and they often manage to create brand loyalty—consumers buying their favorite brand of soap powder or cola, for example, in preference to any of the others on sale. Once this loyalty has been established, a firm may be able to increase the price of its product slightly without losing all of its customers.

Oligopoly

Further away from the competition end of the spectrum is oligopoly, a noun derived from the Greek words *oligos*, meaning "a few," and *poleein*, meaning "to sell." Oligopoly occurs when a few large firms share most of the output of an industry. Examples of oligopolies include the automobile, breakfast cereal, and aerospace industries. Although broadly

similar, such industries can differ widely in detailed characteristics. Some may produce virtually identical products, for example, chemicals, gasoline, or pharmaceuticals. Others may produce highly differentiated products, such as automobiles and computers. The differentiated nature of these products once again introduces the possibility of consumer brand loyalty, which firms make great efforts to exploit.

Thus much of the competition between oligopolists arises from the ways in which their products are marketed—that is, the ways in which they try to persuade consumers to

ABOVE: *Before anyone can drive a yellow cab in New York City, he or she must obtain an operator's license. This is both a barrier to entry into the market and a source of revenue for the authorities.*

buy their produce. Oligopolistic markets are characterized by barriers to entry and the interdependence of firms in the industry.

Barriers to entry

In perfect competition it is easy for new firms to set up as rivals to existing firms because there are no barriers to entry into the marketplace. As a result, high prices and profits are transitory. If firms in a perfectly competitive industry profit through high prices in the short run, in the long run new firms will enter the industry, thus driving down prices and profits. In oligopolies, by contrast, there are typically substantial barriers that slow the entry of new firms and enable existing firms to earn excessive profits in the short and the long runs.

Barriers to entry can be divided into two categories: legal barriers and technical barriers. The extent and effectiveness of these barriers may vary from industry to industry. The following are some of the most important legal barriers.

Patents and copyright

When a firm or individual develops a new product, he, she, or it may apply for legal protection of ownership in the form of a patent or a copyright. A patent conveys the exclusive rights to an invention to its holder for a period of 17 years. Once a patent has expired, anyone may then exploit the invention. For example, Johnson & Johnson formerly owned the patent to acetaminophen, a nonaspirin pain reliever that it marketed under the name Tylenol. When its patent expired, other companies produced and marketed acetaminophen as "Nonaspirin Pain Reliever." It should be noted, however, that only Johnson & Johnson was allowed to use the name Tylenol because that is a registered trademark. Copyrights provide similar legal protection to developers of certain intellectual property, including literature, music, artistic works, and computer software. Tariffs and other trade restrictions, meanwhile, can limit international entrants.

License and franchise

Another legal barrier to entry is a license or franchise granted by a government. Licenses are a condition of entry into many professions, including practising medicine, practising law, driving taxis, harvesting shrimp, hairstyling, and plumbing. Although it is argued that licenses are needed in these professions to protect the public from unscrupulous practitioners, by limiting competition these licenses also lead to higher prices for products or services in these fields.

Natural monopolies

Entry into a market may sometimes be barred by a natural monopoly. A single firm is desirable in certain industries because multiple firms lead to higher costs. Such is the case with public utilities. In this area—a classic natural monopoly—it is common for government to grant an exclusive franchise to one firm, but to regulate the product's price in order to ensure that the firm will not exploit its monopoly power. The government sets the price so that the firm can make a normal rate of return on its investment and nothing more. This regulatory practice is known as average cost pricing and is widely used for pricing public utilities, including electricity and cable television. Sometimes the government has chosen not to grant an exclusive franchise, but rather to provide the service itself. Such is the case with the U.S. Postal Service and often with other goods and services, including water supply and refuse collection. The government uses average cost pricing to price the goods and services it provides. Unlike their private sector counterparts, government enterprises need not make a profit to remain in business. Lacking the profit motive, however, these enterprises have often been criticized for failing to provide the best service at the lowest cost.

Technical barriers

In addition to legal barriers entry to some industries may be impeded by their economic nature and characteristics. Obstacles of this type are known as technical barriers.

Further obstacles to entry may be presented by the ownership or control of factors of production or distribution. For example, suppose an entrepreneur noticed that profits could be made by entering the diamond industry. To do so, he or she would have to acquire the rights to a diamond mine. However, unfortunately for this hopeful newcomer, the De Beers Diamond Corporation already controls 80 percent of the world's diamond mines and will not sell them to any potential competitor. Control of an essential input by a firm or small group of firms can also serve as a barrier to entry to an industry. In addition to the diamond industry control of an essential input has limited the entry of new firms into the nickel, aluminum, sulfur, and oil industries.

Another technical barrier is a threat by an existing firm or firms to reduce their prices if new firms should enter the industry. This practice, known as limit pricing, is most effective if potential entrants regard the threat as

credible and liable to be carried out. A threat to reduce the price of a good is most credible if the existing firms have idle capacity and can easily increase output and cut prices if an interloper seeks entry.

An established firm can also fight for dominance in the market through massive advertising campaigns. Potential entrants cannot hope to match the advertising budget for their own product and so are unable to compete.

The high startup costs and economies of scale typical of heavy industries such as steel and automobile manufacture make it difficult for small firms to become established and compete with existing firms.

ABOVE: In the United Kingdom in the 1990s Hoover offered free flights to the United States to anyone who spent £100 on their products. The acceptance of this promotion was much higher than anticipated, with disastrous consequences for the firm.

OPEC and the theory of cartels

OPEC is the acronym for the Organization of Petroleum Exporting Countries. Its membership includes eleven countries from Africa (Algeria, Libya, and Nigeria), Asia (Indonesia), the Middle East (Iran, Iraq, Kuwait, Qatar, Saudi Arabia, and the United Arab Emirates), and Latin America (Venezuela). The aim of this oil cartel is to manipulate the price of crude oil to the advantage of its members.

A study of OPEC is instructive in understanding the nature of cartels. Economic theory suggests that there is an incentive for cartels to form since the firms in an industry are made better off by colluding with each other to restrict output, raise price, and earn monopoly profits. However, once formed, cartels tend to be unstable. That is because each member of a cartel has an incentive to cheat on the organization by increasing its own output. If too many members of a cartel cheat, the agreement breaks down, output increases, and prices and profits fall. This suggests that cartels are most effective when: (a) only a small number of firms is involved; (b) it is easy to detect and punish cheaters; and (c) barriers to entry exist to limit competition from outside of the cartel.

As the theory predicted, OPEC has had a difficult time maintaining high oil prices. The history of OPEC is one of repeated agreements by member nations to restrict output and raise prices, followed by cheating on the agreement. OPEC has also had to deal with increased oil production from non-OPEC members Mexico, the United Kingdom, and Norway.

ABOVE: Sheikh Yamani of Saudi Arabia at a meeting of OPEC, the mighty cartel of (mainly Middle Eastern) oil-producing nations.

Other barriers

The following are some of the other barriers that might discourage a new firm from entering an established market:
● Brand loyalty. New entrants into a market find that customers remain loyal to a particular supplier and that, in order to compete, they must—at least to begin with—supply at prices below the established firm's costs. Brand loyalty is often reinforced by advertising, another costly undertaking that may also deter competitors.
● Lower costs for an established firm. Established firms will have developed production and marketing skills, whereas a newcomer will have to pay more for them at the outset.
● Mergers and takeovers. Existing firms may buy up or amalgamate with new entrants into the market, thereby removing any possible threat to their own dominance.

● Intimidation. Both legal and illegal forms of harassment may be used against unwanted intruders in an established market.

Interdependence of firms

Because there are by definition only a few firms in an oligopolistic market, each firm has to take account of the others' actions. They are thus said to be interdependent. If one firm changes the price of its product, for example, then the demand for that product will be directly affected. An increase in price will generally result in a fall in sales, while a price cut will cause sales to increase. In the case of a reduction in price the firm's rivals might respond either by holding their prices at the same level as before or by reducing them in order to compete. Therefore, in an oligopolistic market it is essential that all firms remain aware of, and are able to anticipate, the actions of their competitors.

Collusion

Studies of collusion have been made in many countries. One such undertaking, by researchers at the University of Essex in the United Kingdom, used data from British manufacturing industries during the 1950s. It was found that at this time around half the British manufacturing sector was involved in agreements significantly affecting competition. Although they were, in the most part, not illegal, they were also not enforceable at law.

It was found that collusion was less likely in industries with a high advertising expenditure. There was also weak evidence to suggest that collusion was less likely to occur in organizations with high expenditures on research and development. The more capital intensive the industry—that is, the more it depended on machinery rather than labor—the more likely it was that collusion would take place. The rate of growth of the turnover (earnings) of the organizations was also found to be an influential factor. Firms with very high or very low rates of growth were unlikely to collude. On the other hand, firms with a moderate rate of growth would be much more likely to do so.

Cartels

The interdependence of firms in an oligopolistic market results in them taking one of two courses of action. They may either decide to collude with each other, or alternatively they could compete with each other to try and increase their share of the total market. Colluding with each other means that they make joint decisions and act together. As a result, they effectively become a larger monopolistic organization, which is sometimes known as a cartel.

Collusion can result in the firms reaching agreement on price, market share, advertising, and other business strategies of mutual interest. If firms reach a formal agreement, then the resulting organization is known as a cartel (see box on facing page).

The lower the costs of entry to and exit from a market in terms of barriers to entry, such as advertising, the more difficult it will become for oligopolists to collude or make excessive profits. If cartels are formed, however, then new entrants to the market will be discouraged. This is because, in order to maintain its competitive position, a cartel can set up, for example, a new common research laboratory or buy up the entire means of distribution. However, because a perfectly contestable market has no costs of entry or exit, advocates of free competition will argue that perfectly contestable markets must be in the public interest, since they reduce the chance of collusion and are thus to the benefit of the consumer.

Informal collusion

Very often each member of a cartel will be given a sales quota, which is a specific amount of goods that it can sell before allowing orders to be passed on to other members of the cartel. Collusion of this type need not be formal. Informal collusion includes tacit agreements by which the firms in an oligopoly make sure that they do not engage in activities such as price-cutting or excessive advertising. Unwritten rules may exist among the firms in the industry. Sometimes firms will follow the leadership of a dominant firm in making marketing decisions. Alternatively, there may be an informal agreement between the participants about how general market conditions should affect pricing strategies. It is easy to see how these activities may be in the interests of the firms but not necessarily to the benefit of the consumer.

Theories of oligopoly

Through extensive case studies economists have developed a number of theories that help predict the behavior of firms operating in oligopolistic markets.

In 1939 economists Paul Sweezy, R.L. Hall, and C.J. Hitch developed a theory of non-collusive oligopoly. It was an attempt to explain the behavior of firms in an oligopoly when they competed with each other.

Kinked demand curve

This theory became known as the kinked demand curve theory. The kink in the demand curve is at the current price. The demand curve is illustrated in Figure 1 on page 94.

If the firm raises its price from P_1, then it will lose demand for its product. The curve in the diagram is relatively elastic above the kink. This means that a more than proportionate quantity will be lost relative to the price rise. Other firms will not follow suit to gain this lost trade from the firm. If a firm lowers its price from P_1, then the demand curve is relatively inelastic—this is because it is steeper. Rivals will follow suit and cut their price to avoid losing business. By cutting its price, the firm will not gain an increased market share.

One big criticism of the kinked demand curve theory is that it does not account for how the price is set in the first place. It is also complicated and therefore less reliable in times of high inflation, when all prices are rising. During such periods oligopolists would have to raise prices in order to compensate for increases in their own costs.

Game theory

An alternative explanation of oligopoly is game theory, which was originally formulated in 1944 by the mathematicians John von Neumann and Oskar Morgenstern. Game theory attacks the easy assumptions of inter-dependence by taking as its premise the expectation that a firm's rivals will behave ingeniously in response to competition. Thus game theory is a method of studying the various alternative strategies that oligopolists may choose to adopt depending on their assumptions about their rivals' behavior. The example outlined below is known as a simple dominant strategy game. Consider two firms (X and Y) that produce identical products in a single market and have the same costs and demand for their product. The table (below) shows the different profits that they could make under four different strategies, A, B, C, and D.

If we assume that firm X and firm Y are both charging $2 and so following strategy A, they each make a profit of $10 million. The total market profit is therefore $20 million.

Now let us assume that both firms independently consider reducing their prices to $1.80. Before making this decision, each firm must take cognizance of the possible consequences of their decision in terms of what its rival might do. Firm X knows that its rival, Y, might react in one of two ways—it could either lower its own price to $1.80, or it could maintain it at $2.

If Firm X were cautious, it would try to anticipate what Y might do. If X kept its price at $2, the worst thing for X would be if Y cut its price. This would be strategy C. X's profit would then fall to $5 million.

If X were to reduce its price, then the worst thing would again be if Y cut its price, but this time X's profit only falls to $8 (strategy D). If X is cautious, it will cut its price. If Y, too, is cautious, it will also cut its price to $1.80. This approach is known as a maximin policy: it maximizes the minimum profits possible.

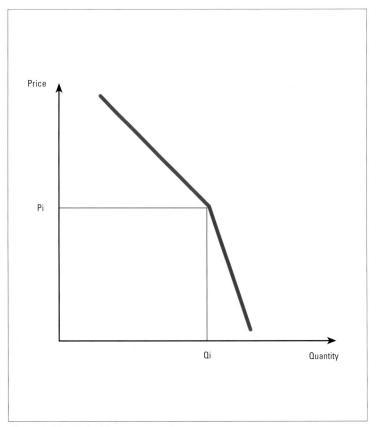

Figure 1 The kinked demand curve.

Another possible strategy is that known as the optimistic approach. In this scenario X will try to realize the highest profit because it assumes that Y will make decisions that turn out to be favorable to X itself. In this case X again cuts its price but on the optimistic assumption that Y will leave its price unchanged. If X is correct, it will achieve strategy B and make $12 million profit. This is known as a maximax strategy. Because both approaches lead to the same strategy, the game is known as a dominant strategy game.

The prisoner's dilemma is a slightly different game in which two or more firms independently attempt to choose the best strategy for whatever the others are likely to do and end up in a worse position than they would have been in the first place.

			X's Price			
			$2			$1.80
Y's Price	$2	A	$10m each		B	$5m for Y $12m for X
	$1.80	C	$12m for Y $5m for X		D	$8m each

Table 1 Different strategies of firms X and Y and profits that result from each.

Advertising

One of the most important areas in which oligopolists will attempt to predict each other's actions is in advertising policy. Advertising brings information to potential consumers and may be a necessary aid to the successful introduction of a new product into the marketplace. In addition, advertising aids research and development by publicizing new features of a product and can encourage price competition. Since sales are likely to increase as a result of advertising, advertising can help bring about economies of scale.

Advertising is necessary only because the markets are imperfect. In the conditions of perfect competition outlined at the start of this chapter firms and consumers would have perfect knowledge, and advertising would therefore not be needed. But in the real world the objective of the advertiser is not simply to disseminate the information that will provide potential purchasers with perfect knowledge—the advertiser may also seek to influence the customer by making various claims and value judgments about the product.

Advertising of this type is controversial because it tries to persuade people to buy rather than just inform them of the basic minimum facts and leave them to make objective decisions. According to critics, this creates wants and contributes to scarcity, thereby increasing it. It also increases materialism and uses resources that could be usefully applied elsewhere. Advertising can also raise prices because it introduces new costs, and it can create a barrier to entry to new firms. In fact, advertising is often likely to be the largest and most important barrier to entry, since new firms may not be able to afford large advertising programs of their own. Environmental objectors point to unsightly or even offensive billboards that represent a cost to society.

Price discrimination

So far it has been assumed that the oligopolist or monopolist will charge only a single price for his or her product. Monopolistic power results in both types of firm being able to charge different prices in different markets: this is known as price discrimination.

ABOVE: The billboards in Times Square, New York, draw the attention of passersby to a wide range of products but are condemned as eyesores by some critics.

The conditions necessary for the successful operation of price discrimination are:

● The firm must be able to set its own prices.
● The markets must be separate. No market must be able to resell to any other.
● Each market must have a different sensitivity to changes in price—that is, different price elasticities of demand. Price elasticity of demand (PED) measures the amount that a change in the price of a product affects demand for that product, all other factors remaining constant. PED is defined as the percentage change in quantity demanded that is produced by a one percent change in price. The higher price will be charged in the less price-elastic market.

Degrees of discrimination

Among the best-known and most widely practiced forms of price discrimination are the following:

● First-degree price discrimination, when the seller tries to get the maximum price from each consumer.
● Second-degree price discrimination, when discriminating firms charge each of their customers on a sliding scale based on the amount of the product that he or she is purchasing. For example, a power utility may charge more per

unit for the first few kilowatts of electricity used than for subsequent units.

● In third degree price discrimination consumers are divided into different market segments (often defined by income), and each is charged a different price. A well-known example is airlines, which charge one rate to first-class passengers and another to tourists.

Multinationals and international trade

Many firms operate in markets where they have to enter into international trade in order to remain competitive. Alternatively, further expansion might involve a firm looking to overseas markets for new outlets. There is virtual agreement among economists and politicians that everybody benefits from trade. International trade is now encouraged by organizations such as the General Agreement on Trades and Tariffs (GATT) and the World Trade Organization (WTO).

The reasoning behind this belief has its foundations in the work of 18th-century economist Adam Smith, who maintained that output would be higher if workers specialized in a single task, a concept known as division of labor. Similarly, world trade increases, and every country will be better off if each produces what it is best at producing, and all countries trade with each other. If one country can produce a good using fewer resources than another country, it is said to have an absolute advantage. If it can produce a good at a lower opportunity cost (*see page 81*), it is said to have a comparative advantage. In other words, a country with a comparative advantage can produce a given amount of a good and incur lower costs for the resources it has used than the other countries.

Firms have traditionally been owned by nationals of one country and have either specialized in supplying their home market or have become involved with importing and exporting products and raw materials. The nature of modern trading has led to the proliferation of multinational corporations. This is partly a result of the numerous mergers that have taken place since the end of World War II, many of which have involved firms of one country taking over or being taken over by firms from another. The original aim of firms in becoming multinationals was to acquire more resources or markets, or to reduce transportation costs.

Labor-spreading devices

Such huge multinational corporations will typically locate various aspects of production, marketing, accounts, and research in different countries depending on the local costs. By doing this they are able to exploit price differences to their advantage, usually carrying out different stages of production in the country that has the cheapest resources. For example, many multinationals have turned to the Far East in search of cheap labor. An early choice was Japan, but in recent decades the search has broadened out to embrace other Southeast Asian countries, where production processes can be carried out at a fraction of what they would cost in the west.

BELOW: Electricity users may be charged more for the first few units they consume than for later purchases. This is an example of second-degree price discrimination.

LEFT: The Saab car company is so strongly associated with its native Sweden that many of its customers may still be unaware that the firm is now a subsidiary of General Motors, the U.S. automobile multinational.

The manufacture of domestic appliances such as televisions was traditionally a labor-intensive task. This means that the many stages involved in producing the items were concentrated in a single factory. When the Dutch multinational electronics firm Philips transferred its head office to Singapore, this was in recognition of the fact that 80 percent of its laborforce was in Southeast Asia. However, despite this move, current labor costs in domestic electronic equipment assembled in Europe actually amount to only 10 percent of total costs. But now that the commitment has been made, it might be too expensive for firms like Philips to withdraw.

As multinational corporations continue to grow in size and number, so too do the controversies surrounding them. Many argue that domestic jobs are lost as firms locate abroad and take advantage of cheap labor. At the same time, the host country may suffer if the multinational forces local producers out of the market, so reducing competition and consumer choice.

Others contend that firms being involved overseas opens up new sources of information and export markets for the foreign country; the country may increase in wealth as a consequence. In addition, costs of overseas work increase as the foreign workers become better organized. Very often countries with low labor costs have poor standards of health and inadequate safety requirements. Again, it might be argued that as labor becomes more organized and better skilled, increasing pressure is brought on employers to raise these standards. Recent statistics have actually shown that multinationals now pay their workers more than the average in the host country, create jobs faster, and spend heavily on research and development.

According to United Nations estimates, in 1998 there were 53,607 multinationals controlling a total of 448,917 foreign-affiliated firms. Many of the biggest and most important multinationals are of U.S. origin (*see* table on page 99). In the United Kingdom this type of company plays a more influential role in the country's economy than in that of any other advanced nation. Firms such as the Ford Motor Corporation are so strongly established in the United Kingdom that Britons may now have difficulty in thinking of them as foreign.

International currencies

There are two main ways in which trading between countries differs from internal trade. One is that goods must pass through international boundaries and are therefore subject to the laws and taxation rules that govern imports and exports. The second is that payment for goods involves the use of foreign currencies.

Ideally, firms in any country prefer to be paid for products and services in their own currency. Although many of the world's

SEE ALSO:

- Volume 3, page 43: Government and business

- Volume 4, page 6: The U.S. government and world economics

- Volume 4, page 63: The world economy

- Volume 5, page 74: Monopoly

- Volume 5, page 78: Oligopoly and oligopolistic competition

- Volume 5, page 93: Regulation and antitrust laws

- Volume 6, page 86: The West in the 20th century

currencies, particularly the U.S. dollar and the German Deutsche mark, are internationally acceptable, local currency payments, though unwanted, are often unavoidable. In some circumstances this may mean that money earned in a particular country must remain in that country and can thus be used only for reinvestment. This option could be of lasting benefit to a developing country but is not necessarily desirable to the multinational, which may choose not to locate in a country if it cannot export its profits.

Rates of exchange

Like any other commodity that is being traded, currencies acquire a price in terms of each other. This price is known as the rate of exchange. A new currency now appearing on the international markets is the euro, the coinage of the EU. At present not all members of the EU are using the euro, and the question of whether or not to adopt it is particularly controversial in some countries such as the United Kingdom.

Theoretical models have been created to explain many aspects of the real markets in which firms operate. There now is a strong tendency for firms to become larger as mergers take place. Many of these mergers are multinational. At the same time, governments, fearful of the growing power and influence of monopolies, introduce laws to protect competition, which is still seen as the most efficient form of market.

ABOVE: The rate at which one nation's currency may be exchanged for that of another may have a profound effect on levels of trade and tourism.

MULTINATIONALS (in decreasing size of total assets)

Company	Country of origin	Industry
General Electric	U.S.	Electronics
Shell, Royal Dutch	U.S.	Petroleum
Ford Motor Co.	U.S.	Automotives
Exxon Corp.	U.S.	Petroleum
General Motors	U.S.	Automotives
IBM	U.S.	Computers
Toyota	Japan	Automotives
Volkswagen Group	Germany	Automotives
Mitsubishi Corp.	Japan	Diversified
Mobil Corp.	U.S.	Petroleum

Source: UNCTAD World Investment Report 1998: Trends and Determinants. Geneva, Switzerland

Market failures and externalities

Market failure occurs when resources are allocated inefficiently. In some cases producers may have no incentive to provide a particular good. One of the goals of economic theory is to discover ways of successfully avoiding or rectifying such an undesirable state of affairs.

Modern economic theory states that if markets are perfectly competitive, scarce resources will be allocated efficiently to consumers and producers alike. Market failure is said to occur when markets fail to achieve allocative efficiency (see below). This failure might occur as a result of imperfect competition in markets and anticompetitive practices by firms (*see* How firms behave in the real world, page 80). So, for example, the allocation of a product will not be efficient if only one firm is producing it and is able to charge consumers a high price to purchase it.

Market failure will also occur in the case of public goods, such as law and order, and mixed or merit goods, such as education, which will either be underprovided by the market mechanism, or—in the case of public goods—not provided at all. So, for example, nobody can be excluded from benefiting from the provision of policing in an area, with the result that the incentive to pay is reduced, and there is little reason for private firms to provide this service.

Externalities

The other major incidence of market failure may be seen when there are externalities present—that is, when costs or benefits arise from an economic activity and fall on a third party. In this case the full costs or benefits of an activity such as pumping raw sewage into the sea fall on people in general rather than on the individual or firm engaged in that particular activity. It does not cost the firm anything to pollute a stretch of coastline—the costs of its activities are borne by the environment, by the people who suffer the effects of a dirty beach, and by fishermen who can no longer fish in the area.

Economists study the degree to which economic efficiency is reduced by market failures such as anticompetitive practices, public goods, and externalities so that they can judge what action can be taken to correct these failures and improve efficiency.

Economic efficiency

In his magnum opus *The Wealth of Nations* Adam Smith observed that participants in market economies serve not only their own interests but also are led as if by an "invisible hand" toward the best interest of society.

ABOVE: If one firm pollutes the ocean, this action may have a detrimental effect on other firms that catch and sell fish. This is known as a negative externality.

Building on Smith's ideas, later economists have defined an allocation of resources as being in society's best interest if it maximizes the value of those resources. Such an allocation is said to be economically efficient. An allocation of resources is economically efficient if it is impossible to make one person better off without leaving someone else worse off. Conversely, if it is possible to make one person better off without leaving anyone else worse off, the allocation of resources is said to be inefficient.

Marginal social benefit

The benefit that society derives from producing one more unit than before of a particular commodity (or good) is referred to as the marginal social benefit. It includes the benefit to the buyer and any indirect benefits gained by other members of society. The price of a good often reflects the willingness of society to pay for it, and thus a good's price is often used as a convenient shorthand for its marginal social benefit. For example, if the price of a ticket to a movie is $6, people paying this price reveal that they value the movie at no less than $6—if they valued the ticket at less than this price, they would not buy it. Some moviegoers will undoubtedly value the movie at more than $6, but there will be some customers who value the movie at exactly $6 and not a penny more.

The economically efficient level of production of a good is found by comparing its marginal social benefit to its marginal social cost. The marginal social cost is the cost to society of producing one additional unit of output, including the costs borne by the producer and other costs incurred indirectly by other members of society. If the marginal social benefit exceeds the marginal social cost, society realizes a net benefit by producing more of the good. If, for example, the marginal social benefit of a video game cartridge is $20, and the marginal social cost of the cartridge is $12, it is economically efficient to produce the cartridge because a net benefit of $8 ($20-$12=$8) is generated by so doing. An economically efficient allocation of resources exploits all opportunities of this type. Conversely, if the marginal social benefit of a good is less than its marginal social cost, society benefits if less of the good is produced. In this situation resources are not being employed in their highest valued use. Suppose, for example, that society values the resources needed to produce a surfboard at $169, but values the surfboard at only $152. It would thus be to the detriment of society if $169 worth of resources were to be converted into a good worth only $152. Society will thus lose $17 worth of resources if the surfboard is produced.

To summarize, society benefits by increasing its production of goods for as long as the marginal social benefit of so doing exceeds the marginal social cost, and by decreasing production of goods with a marginal social benefit that is less than the marginal social cost. The economically efficient level of

ABOVE: In economic terms the amount of money a person will pay to see a movie is no less than that movie's marginal social benefit.

The efficiency of perfectly competitive markets

Economic theory shows that market economies are capable of allocating resources efficiently if industries are perfectly competitive. An industry is said to be perfectly competitive when there are many individual consumers and small firms; each firm produces exactly the same good; there is complete resource mobility; there are no barriers to entering or leaving the industry; consumers and firms have perfect information; and consumers and firms reap all the benefits and bear all the costs of their actions (*see* Competition, expansion, and growth, page 62; *see* How firms behave in the real world, page 80).

To see how a perfectly competitive industry is economically efficient, economists look at the behavior of particular firms. Under perfect competition each firm is assumed to be a profit-maximizer. Because all firms are small in relation to the market as a whole, they find that the market price is beyond their control when making economic decisions.

Although competitive firms accept the price of their good as a given, they are nevertheless capable of adjusting their output levels in order to maximize profit. The way to maximize profit is to adjust the level of output until marginal revenue is equal to marginal cost. Marginal revenue is the additional revenue generated by producing one more unit of a good. Marginal cost is the additional cost incurred through the production of one more unit of the good. If marginal revenue exceeds marginal cost, profit-maximizers will compensate by increasing output. If marginal revenue is less than marginal cost, profit-maximizers will reduce output. The profit-maximizing level of output is found where firms seek neither to increase nor decrease output. This occurs when marginal revenue is equal to marginal cost (see How a business works, page 28).

In perfectly competitive industries firms produce the economically efficient level of output. (Remember that the economically efficient level of output is reached when the marginal social benefit—or its proxy, the price of the good—is equal to the marginal social cost.) For competitive firms marginal revenue and the price of the good are equal because the additional revenue derived from producing one more unit of the good is simply the price handed over by the purchasers. Because the firms bear all of the costs of production in perfect competition, the firm's marginal cost is the marginal social cost. Thus, by equating marginal revenue to marginal cost in the pursuit of profit, firms also equate marginal social benefit to marginal social cost and thereby achieve an economically efficient level of output. What Adam Smith called "the invisible hand" of the market has guided self-interested firms to serve society's best interests.

production of a good is achieved when it is in society's interest neither to increase nor to decrease its current level of production. That is, when the marginal social benefit of a good is exactly equal to its marginal social cost.

Modern economic theory suggests that a market economy has the capacity to allocate resources in a highly desirable manner (*see* box above). But this is based on the assumption that the economy is characterized by perfectly competitive industries. The problem remains: Will the outcome be as desirable if the economy is made up of industries that are not perfectly competitive? In general, the answer to this question is no. When market economies do not provide goods at economically efficient levels, then there is a market failure. Market failures can come about if any of the requirements for perfect competition are not satisfied. Here we look at two sources of market failure: market failures brought about by the absence of competition, and

LEFT: A surfboard is beneficial to society and worth producing only if it can be sold for more than it costs to produce.

market failures that result when consumers and firms do not bear all the costs of their actions—in other words, when externalities are present.

The inefficiency of imperfectly competitive markets

One of the most striking characteristics of a perfectly competitive industry is that there are many individual consumers and firms. If this is not the case, the market will not produce economically efficient output levels, and the industry is said to be imperfectly competitive (*see* box on page 104).

The typical characteristics that may be noted in perfect competition, oligopoly, and monopoly are summarized in Table 1, below.

Monopolies and other forms of imperfect competition lead to market failures because they produce insufficient output. It will be recalled that an economically efficient level of output is found where the marginal social benefit (or price) equals the marginal social cost. Efficient output occurs without government intervention when markets are perfectly competitive. However, while perfectly competitive firms are price-takers, monopolies and imperfect competitors are price-seekers. This has an important implication for marginal revenue. For price-takers marginal revenue and price are equal. For price-seekers marginal revenue is less than price. The reasons for this and its implications are outlined in Table 2 on page 104.

In general, if there is only a single supplier of a good or a service in the market—or if competition is limited in some other way as a result of barriers to entry or large economies of scale (*see* How firms behave in the real world, page 80)—then an inefficient level of output will be produced at a high price. The monopoly firm, or the firms operating under some other form of imperfect competition, can earn excess or abnormal profits without other firms being able to enter the market to

take advantage of these profits, expand output, and push prices down. As a result of this lack of competition consumers will not only face higher prices than they would in a competitive market, but they will also be denied a choice of whom to buy from and face a reduced choice of products to buy.

Correcting the monopoly market failure

In the United States, between the end of the American Civil War in 1865 and the outbreak of World War I in Europe in 1914 came the age of the so-called robber barons. During this period entrepreneurs formed trusts in many basic industries and exerted monopoly power in order to amass great fortunes for themselves. A trust is defined as an organization of firms that conspires to restrict output and raise prices in order to garner monopoly profits for its members. Trusts were formed in many U.S. industries, including coal, electrical goods, leather, meat packing, oil, railroads, steel, sugar, and tobacco. The only way to limit their power was through legislation.

Trust busters

Concern over the monopoly power thus generated led to the passage of a series of trust-busting laws. The most important U.S. antitrust laws, the Sherman Antitrust Act of 1890, the Clayton Antitrust Act of 1914, and the Federal Trade Commission Act of 1914, prohibited price-fixing and a range of other anticompetitive behaviors and created the Federal Trade Commission (FTC). The U.S. government used these laws to break up trusts in the oil, tobacco, aluminum, and telephone industries. The campaign thus started still continues: in the late 1990s the U.S. government charged Microsoft with unfair business practices (*see* box on page 106).

An increase in merger activity after the end of World War II in 1945 led to the Celler-Kefauver Antimerger Act of 1950. This new legislation gave the FTC additional powers to review proposed mergers and ensure that

Market structure	Number of firms	Power of firms to raise price	Barrier to Entry	Examples
Perfect competition	Many	None	None	Agricultural products provided by many small farms
Oligopoly	Few	Moderate	High	Breakfast cereals, automobiles
Monopoly	One	High	Very high	Utilities

Table 1 The typical characteristics of a firm or firms in perfect competition, oligopoly, and monopoly.

Imperfect competition and economic efficiency

In an imperfectly competitive market firms are price-seekers rather than price-takers. Price-seekers can lower their prices in order to increase sales and hence increase their total revenue. Thus the revenue that a firm earns from selling one more unit of output is equal to the price of the unit sold minus the difference in the price on all of the units that could have been sold at a higher price. For example, suppose that a monopolist sells 100 rubber balls at $10.00 per ball. At this level of output total revenue is $1,000. Now, in order to sell one more ball (101 balls), the seller must reduce the price to (say) $9.98. Total revenue is increased to $1,007.98 ($9.98 x 101), and thus the marginal revenue of the 101st ball is $7.98 ($1,007.98 minus $1,000). Notice that this is less than the price of a single ball ($9.98). Although the firm receives $9.98 from the sale of the 101st ball, it loses $0.02 per ball on the 100 balls that it could have sold for $10.00 each (a total of $2.00). Thus in general, for imperfect competitors marginal revenue is less than price.

To see how levels of output and price may differ between perfect and imperfect competition, suppose that a perfectly competitive industry is suddenly monopolized. The golden rule for profit maximization requires the equating of marginal revenue and marginal cost, so that the revenue received for the last unit of output produced is equal to the cost of producing that last unit. However, since for perfectly competitive firms marginal revenue equals price, this implies that price is equated to marginal cost at the optimal level of output (*see* box on "The efficiency of perfectly competitive markets," page 102). Now imagine that a monopolist takes over the industry and finds that price is equal to marginal cost. To maximize profit, the monopolist will seek to equate marginal revenue to marginal cost. Since marginal revenue is less than price for a monopoly, the monopolist finds that its current level of output is too large—that is, its marginal cost exceeds the monopoly marginal revenue. The monopolist therefore reduces output and simultaneously raises price.

To summarize, because marginal revenue is less than price for a monopolist, it will be in the monopolist's interest to produce less output at a higher price than a competitive firm. This is the market failure that occurs with imperfect competition.

they did not lead to restraints of trade. In recent years the FTC has exercised this power by disallowing several proposed corporate amalgamations. For example, the FTC vetoed the proposed linkup between the Rite Aid and Revco drugstore chains and the Staples and Office Depot office supply chains.

Negative externalities

A negative externality is a cost borne by a third party due to the actions of others, but without the consent of the third party. For example, you might decide to have a party and play some very loud music. But it is not just you and your guests who have to listen to the music. For your neighbors the music that keeps them awake that night is a negative externality.

When negative externalities are present, the marginal social cost exceeds the marginal private cost, and private decision-making leads to too high a level of production and consumption. Consider the example set out in Table 2 below. The price of the good—a proxy for the marginal social benefit—is $50. The marginal private cost is $10 for the first unit, and this increases by $10 for each additional unit. On top of the marginal private cost there is also a marginal external cost of $10 per unit. This $10 may represent the cost of smoke emitted by the firm into the atmosphere or of the effluent pumped into a nearby river or stream. The marginal social cost is the sum of the marginal private cost and the marginal external cost. A competitive firm will select a level of output at which the marginal revenue is equal to the marginal private cost.

Quantity	Marginal social benefit (or price)	Marginal private cost	Marginal external cost	Marginal social cost
1	$50	$10	$10	$20
2	$50	$20	$10	$30
3	$50	$30	$10	$40
4	$50	$40	$10	$50
5	$50	$50	$10	$60
6	$50	$60	$10	$70
7	$50	$70	$10	$80

Table 2 Marginal costs and benefits at varying levels of production.

In making its policy decisions the firm will consider only the private benefits and costs of its actions. An inspection of Table 2 reveals that the firm in this example will produce five units of output.

The road to market failure

The problem here, however, is that such a level of output is not economically efficient. The economically efficient output is found at the point where marginal social benefit equals marginal social cost. Returning to Table 2, we can see that this occurs at four units of output. Note that this level of output is less than the output produced by private decision-makers. Negative externalities mean that too much of the good is produced and consumed, thus causing market failure.

Correcting negative externalities

The correction of the market failures resulting from externalities is one of the main economic roles of government. Externalities may be corrected in three ways: by regulation, by altering economic incentives, or by means of market-based alternatives.

The regulatory approach

The most widely used method of correcting negative externalities is by government regulation. These regulations may take many forms. One type of regulation is known as an emissions standard. Under this type of regulation the emissions of firms are monitored and must be kept below specified levels. Firms may meet the standard either by changing their methods of production or by reducing their output.

Another type of regulation is known as output restriction. As previously noted, negative externalities lead private decision-makers

ABOVE: A pumping station on Lake Okeechobee, Florida. If the water here is not kept clean, negative externalities will result.

BELOW: The benefit of electricity is generally agreed to outweigh the unsightliness of these towers in Houston, Texas.

Is Microsoft a monopoly?

In the short span of only two decades Microsoft grew from a small startup firm to the most valuable corporation in the United States. Its cofounders, Bill Gates and William Allen, rank among the world's richest men. However, hand in hand with Microsoft's financial success have come allegations that the firm has reached its preeminence by engaging in a range of illegal anticompetitive practices.

Among other charges, Microsoft has been accused of: (a) attempting to go through with a merger that would be detrimental to competition (it eventually backed away from its planned amalgamation with Intuit, a competitor in personal finance software, when it appeared that the merger would be disallowed by the Federal Trade Commission); and (b) bullying makers of personal computers (PCs) into licensing the Windows software programs on Microsoft's terms.

Expert economists have testified in this case on behalf of both the U.S. government and the Microsoft Corporation. The government claimed that Microsoft engaged in tying contracts by requiring the appearance of Internet Explorer on every desktop as a condition of licensing Windows 98, and that the firm took unfair advantage of Windows' status as an industry standard to prevent the entry of possible competitors into the market. Microsoft meanwhile has maintained that while it is undoubtedly highly competitive, its success has been achieved not through illegal business practices, but because it provides customers with the products they want.

There is much at stake in this action. Microsoft could be broken up for violating antitrust laws, and such a decision will have far-reaching and deeply serious consequences for the computer industry as a whole.

ABOVE: Bill Gates started the 21st century as chairman of Microsoft and the world's richest person.

to produce too much output. Unlike the emissions standard, this type of regulation reduces emissions indirectly as the firm reduces output. In extreme cases the output might be reduced to zero. A prohibition of output is the path that has been followed to correct the externalities associated with the logging of old growth forests of the Pacific Northwest (*see* box on "Bald eagles and spotted owls," pages 110-111).

Another type of regulatory technique is known as the prescriptive regulation. A prescriptive regulation designates the equipment or methods by which a good may be produced. These prescriptions are not adopted voluntarily by firms because they are not the least costly method (in a private sense) of making the product. By increasing the firms' costs, they reduce the firms' profits. For examples of prescriptive regulations, *see* "Saving the Taj Mahal" on page 112; *see* "Why can't I find a taxi in Kathmandu?" on page 113.

The regulatory approach requires continual policing to ensure that firms comply with the regulations. If the firms fail to comply with the regulations, they are subject to penalties,

typically fines. If the probability of being detected in noncompliance with a regulation is low, and if the penalty for noncompliance is small, firms may choose to ignore the regulations and, if caught in noncompliance, pay the penalty. Thus the sanctions must be strong to be effective.

Many economists are critical of the regulatory approach because they believe that it is unlikely to achieve environmental goals in the least costly way to society. Those who take this view tend to prefer emission control methods that rely on economic incentives or those that are market-based.

Altering economic incentives

Economic incentives can be structured in two ways to reduce emissions. First, firms can be charged an effluent fee or tax for every unit of emission. This approach to emissions control is also known as a Pigovian tax, after British economist A.C. Pigou, who originated the idea in 1920. Ideally, the effluent fee should be set at a level that matches the external cost to society of the emissions. By charging this fee, the external cost is "internalized" by the private decision-maker, and his or her decisions will be economically efficient. Returning once more to the example in Table 2, an effluent fee could be set so that it raises the marginal cost to the firm by $10. With such an increase the firm's marginal cost (the marginal private cost plus the effluent fee) will exactly equal the marginal social cost. With these costs the profit-maximizing firm will produce the economically efficient four units of output.

The second method of reducing emissions is by rewarding firms that take their own initiatives to conform. Using this method, a subsidy is paid to a firm for each unit by which it reduces emissions. In this scenario firms are faced with a choice between two possible courses of action: they must decide whether it is more profitable for them to keep up their current levels of emissions and receive no subsidy or to reduce emissions by curtailing output or adopting cleaner methods of production. In the latter case they would commit themselves to collecting profit from the remaining output and payments from the government. Thus the subsidy rate, if set at ideal levels, will internalize the external cost of emissions. With a subsidy system an opportunity cost to the firm of a unit of emissions is the subsidy that they forego by producing that emission.

One advantage of effluent fees and emissions-reduction subsidies is that they are less costly to society than regulations. This is because firms on which a regulatory approach is imposed must comply with the regulations regardless of the cost. Thus some high-cost emission reduction may occur while lower-cost emission reduction does not take place. Neither effluent fees nor emissions-reduction subsidies suffer from the same limitations: in both cases the firms themselves select which sources of emissions they will reduce or eliminate. Profit-maximizers will first reduce those sources of emissions that are the least costly. They proceed to more costly methods of emission reduction only after low-cost methods of emission reduction have been fully exploited. In spite of this great advantage, effluent fees and emission-reduction subsidies have not been widely used to date in the United States.

Externalities and property rights

Professor Garrett Hardin, in his classic 1968 article "The Tragedy of the Commons," recast the problem of negative externalities as one of common property. Common property is defined as property for which clear ownership rights have not been established. Common property belongs to no one individual and is therefore available to everyone. Examples of common property include the air, the oceans,

ABOVE: *African rhinos are seen as a common property resource in economics. Because they belong to no one individual, they are in danger of exploitation.*

and the rivers. Pacific salmon, African rhinoceros, and South American macaws are also common property resources.

If these resources were private property, their owners would naturally require compensation (payment) for their use. However, since they are common property, they are regarded as free goods by consumers and firms alike. Common property is therefore destined for excessive exploitation simply because it is free and no one is necessarily accountable or responsible for it. The dangers implicit in this excessive use are what Hardin dramatically referred to in the title of his article. This problem of common property explains why the air, oceans, and rivers have become so polluted, and why wildlife has become endangered in many parts of the world—what belongs to everybody belongs to nobody.

Market-based alternatives

The argument that negative externalities arise because there is no clear ownership of resources also hints at a possible solution to the problem. The idea is that if the market failures associated with negative externalities are a result of poorly defined property rights (as is the case with common property), establishing and enforcing property rights might solve the problem. The notion that the private market may not misallocate resources in the presence of externalities is known as the Coase Theorem, after Ronald Coase, the Nobel Laureate who first proposed it in 1960.

From the application of the Coase Theorem has developed a new approach to the problem of externalities that utilizes licenses known as transferable permits. The use of transferable permits is a market-based solution to the externality problem that creates property rights where they did not previously exist. The transferable permit approach has now been widely adopted and is used to address problems in pollution and fishery and wildlife management (*see* box on "Trading the Right to Pollute," page 116).

Transferable permit systems, as exemplified in fishery management, work in the following way: the government first determines the desired catch, then issues a number of permits that would allow only the desired catch. Next, the government distributes these permits to the public. Permits may be allocated on a pro-rata basis to existing fishers—a practice known as grandfathering—or auctioned to the highest bidder. Interestingly, the manner of this distribution does not affect the final economic outcome as long as the permits are transferable.

Because the permits are transferable, they will ultimately find their way into the hands of the most efficient fishers. Inefficient fishers holding permits will find that they can earn more by selling their permits to more efficient fishers than by using them themselves. Entry to the fishery is not prohibited. Individuals seeking to enter the fishery may do so simply by purchasing permits. Although initiatives of this type to correct externalities are relatively new, they hold tremendous promise for increased use in the future.

Emissions offsets

The use of emissions offsets is another increasingly popular method of correcting externalities through control of property rights. Under a program of emissions offsets, if an emitter seeks to expand its operations and emissions in an area, it must reduce emissions from another source by an equal amount. For example, suppose that an oil refinery seeks to expand its operations at a plant that will result in 100 more units of emissions than it generated before. Under an emissions-offsets program the firm must reduce emissions elsewhere in the region by 100 units before it is allowed to proceed. This may be accomplished by scaling back existing operations until 100 units of emissions have been eliminated. In reviewing its own operations, the refinery will find that some of its

emissions lead ultimately to higher profits, while others lead to lower profits. The refinery will naturally decide to reduce emissions from those sources where the profitability is less than the profitability of the proposed expansion. This is a more efficient use of the emissions, since society receives better value given the level of emissions.

If the refinery cannot find a source of emissions to scale back within its own organization, it may go outside itself and seek to influence another firm. In such a situation the refinery might buy another business with a view to scaling its competitor back or possibly shutting it down altogether. The refinery will find this profitable if it can generate more revenue from its expanded operations than from the acquired business.

The same methods of control can be used to regulate new firms seeking to enter a certain area for the first time. These businesses will be allowed to come into the market only if they can reduce emissions elsewhere in the region. One of the most important consequences of the emissions-offsets method of emission control is that, like the transferable permit approach, it creates property rights where they did not previously exist. In the case of emissions offsets the property rights to emissions belong to existing firms. These

ABOVE: A cigarette may cause terminal illness not only to the smoker but also to nonsmokers who have to breathe the fumes. This is a negative externality.

firms can continue to emit, or they may sell the rights to these emissions to another business. Of course, the latter will happen only if another business calculates that it can use the emissions rights more profitably than the existing firm.

Although emissions offsets as described above maintain pollution at existing levels, a slight variation on the same basic theme may be used to reduce existing emissions by requiring that the offset exceed the planned increase in emissions. For example, in famously smogbound areas like Los Angeles, California, which fail to meet the federal air quality standards, U.S. law now requires that new sources of emissions must retire—that is, cut back on emission elsewhere—by as much as 120 percent of planned new emissions.

Natural resource economics

The earth's natural resources can be divided into two categories—nonrenewable and renewable. Examples of nonrenewable resources include fossil fuels—e.g., coal, oil, and natural gas—and other minerals—e.g., copper, gold, iron, silver, and uranium. Once

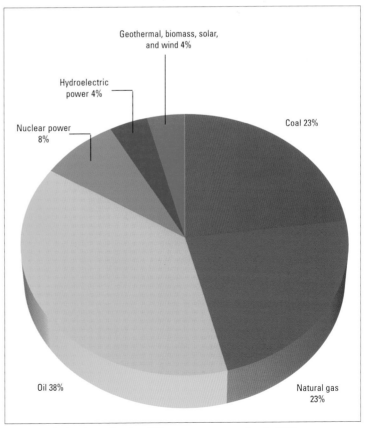

Figure 1: A pie chart showing U.S. energy consumption in 1998.

Bald eagles and spotted owls

ABOVE: Cutting down trees may benefit the human economy, but it has threatened the very existence of the spotted owl.

What do bald eagles and spotted owls have in common? They are both North American birds that were once more common but have recently come close to extinction. The reasons for the decline of these species are different, but there is a common theme.

The bald eagle (*Haliaeetus leucocephalus*) became the national symbol of the United States shortly after the Revolutionary War in 1782. At that time it was estimated that there were as many as 75,000 nesting pairs in the country. By the early 1960s, however, the number of nesting pairs had been reduced to fewer than 450. The demise of the bald eagle is generally attributed to its having been exposed to the long-lived pesticide dichloro-diphenyl-trichloroethane (DDT). DDT—which had been intended to kill insects and increase agricultural productivity—eventually found its way along the food chain into fish, a favorite prey of the bald eagle.

The northern spotted owl (*Strix occidentalis caurina*) is a medium-sized nocturnal bird found only in old-growth forests of the Pacific Northwest. Little is known about the number of nesting pairs of spotted owls that once inhabited the Douglas fir forests, but recent inventories have found as few as several thousand pairs, with the population dropping rapidly. Its numbers have been reduced through the destruction of its habitat by logging activities.

In economic terms the common theme is that the demise of these birds has been caused by negative externalities. The endangerment of the bald eagle is an external cost associated with the use of poisonous insecticide. The great reduction in the number of spotted owls is an external cost of logging in virgin forests. Both species are now protected by federal laws making it

ABOVE: While the country of which it is an emblem has flourished, the bald eagle was once close to extinction.

illegal to kill or harass them. The bald eagle was originally protected by the Bald Eagle Act of 1940 and later by the Endangered Species Act of 1973. The National Forest Management Act of 1976 and the Endangered Species Act protect spotted owls.

Although the verdict is not yet in on the spotted owl, these laws have been successful in facilitating the recovery of the bald eagle. It is believed that there are now more than 5,000 pairs of nesting bald eagles, and the bird was removed from the list of protected species in July 1999.

These successes have not been achieved without cost. The resurgence of the bald eagle has generally been attributed to the banning of DDT in 1972. Although other pesticides have been developed in its place, the time and effort associated with shifting to these alternatives were costly to society. The fight to save the spotted owl and its habitat has led the U.S. courts to halt logging in old-growth forests at great cost to logging communities in the states of California, Oregon, and Washington.

Has all this preservation effort been worthwhile and in the best interest of the American people? Economists attempt to answer this question by analyzing whether the benefits from species preservation exceed the costs thereby incurred. Of course, assessing the benefits is no easy matter. Quite apart from any uncertainty about what effect the extinction of a species may have on the food chain, and hence on the environment as a whole, it might plausibly be argued that it is impossible to put a value on what is essentially an ethical question—the benefit to future generations of living in a world where there is diversity of life.

Saving the Taj Mahal

ABOVE: The beautiful white marble of the Taj Mahal is under serious threat from air pollution.

India's Taj Mahal, one of the world's most famous landmarks, is in danger. In recent years the marble walls of this magnificent structure have been discolored by air polluted by hundreds of coal-fired factories in the region.

The smoke from these factories and the resulting air pollution are an example of a negative externality. The factories do not bear all of the costs of their enterprises. Because the air is common property, they used it freely to emit smoke. By emitting smoke, they have imposed costs on the citizens of the region and damaged the Taj Mahal. The level of factory output and the level of air pollution both exceed economically efficient levels.

The Supreme Court of India has recently taken action to correct this market failure. The Supreme Court has ruled that coal-burning factories in the region must switch from coal to cleaner natural gas or relocate from the region. This prescriptive regulation, if enforced, will improve air quality, but not without cost to the region's factories and factory workers.

Benefit-cost analysis can be used to determine if this policy is in the best interest of the Indian people. This analytical technique requires a direct comparison of the benefits and the costs of a government policy or project. The benefits of pollution reduction include the improved health of the citizens of the region and the preservation of the tourist industry associated with the Taj Mahal. These benefits are compared to the costs born by the coal-fired industries of the region. If the benefits of the policy exceed the costs, then the Supreme Court's remedy is in the best interest of the Indian people. Conversely, if the costs exceed the benefits, then the policy leaves the Indian people worse off.

a nonrenewable resource has been used, it cannot by definition be replaced. Examples of renewable resources include fisheries, forests, livestock, and alternative energy sources such as solar power and wind power—they can be regenerated by careful husbandry.

The United States relies heavily on nonrenewable resources, especially coal, oil, and natural gas, to generate power (*see* Figure 1, page 109). At the current rates of consumption many environmentalists are concerned that these resources will soon be completely exhausted.

By contrast, however, the economic theory of mineral depletion predicts that these resources will never be fully exhausted. This idea was first put forward in 1931 by economist Harold Hotelling, who noted that as a mineral is depleted, its supply must necessarily decrease. This leads to an increase in the

Why can't I find a taxi in Kathmandu?

ABOVE: *Taxis like this were banned by the government of Nepal in an attempt to reduce pollution in the capital, Kathmandu.*

Increasing levels of air pollution in Kathmandu, the capital of Nepal, have led the government to take drastic measures. A major source of smog in the city is a diesel-powered, three-wheeled vehicle known as a "tempo," vast numbers of which have been in use as taxis. The first action taken by the Nepalese government was to ban the import of further tempos. When this failed to reduce their number, the government banned the use of tempos as taxis altogether. The 1,400 taxi drivers who drove tempos must now either change to cleaner vehicles or exit the industry. This prescriptive regulation has reduced the supply of taxis in Kathmandu and will undoubtedly lead to higher taxi prices. Government regulations to reduce emissions often have the effect of increasing product prices.

Source: "A Shortage of Taxis in Nepal," The Economist, August 7, 1999.

price of the mineral, a rise that has three important consequences. First, at the higher price people will use less of the mineral than they did before. This is the economic law of demand applied to mineral consumption. Second, the higher mineral price will lead people to search for more of the mineral. Finally, the higher price will lead people to seek out substitutes (*see* box, page 114).

Lessons of the oil crisis

Hotelling's predictions have to a large extent been borne out by what has occurred in the oil industry since the end of World War II in 1945. In the 1950s the price of crude oil was low—around $3 per barrel. In the early 1970s, however, political tensions in the Middle East led to the formation of the Organization of Petroleum Exporting Countries (OPEC). The main members of this cartel were oil-rich Arab states. These countries were determined to earn greater revenue from their main export and also to punish the United States and the coun-tries of Western Europe for supporting Israel in the Yom Kippur War of October 1973 against Egypt and Syria.

The growing power of OPEC soon led to much higher crude oil prices. The price peaked at over $30 per barrel for a short time and cur-rently stands at about $20 per barrel. The sudden rise in the cost of crude oil contributed to a worldwide recession and led to much higher retail gasoline prices. In only a short time consumers in North Americans responded by changing from their large traditional gas-guzzling automobiles to smaller, more fuel-effi-cient vehicles. The higher oil price also led to a worldwide search and exploration for previ-ously unexploited sources of crude oil. In addi-tion, wells that had been abandoned as unprof-itable when the price of oil was only $3 per barrel were now reworked and brought back on line at the higher price. Oil was discovered in inhospitable areas like the Alaskan North Slope and the North Sea, and eventually brought to market.

Costing the earth?

ABOVE: It is now important to dispose of domestic and industrial refuse in a way that causes as little damage as possible to the environment.

Since the early 1970s there has been a wide and vigorous debate within the international community about whether or not there are "limits to growth." The issue seems crucial, particularly in the face of rapid population growth in many parts of the world. Can consumers go on consuming and producers go on producing ever-increasing quantities of goods and services—more food and drink, more clothing and cosmetics, more books and newspapers, more automobiles, more televisions, more computers? Or are there in fact strictly defined limits to the resources available from which businesses and firms can produce these things? Perhaps equally important, are there limits to the amounts of pollution and waste—by-products of these production processes—that the earth's environment can absorb? Can the human race carry on in the same way as it has always behaved now that people have learned to split the atom and can now release into the ecosystem potentially lethal radioactive materials that can neither be controlled nor destroyed?

Doomsday scenarios

The debate—which involves governments, businesses, economists, scientists, nongovernmental organizations, and concerned environmentalists—initially revolved around the question of energy. As more and more motorized road vehicles are manufactured and bought, they require more gasoline to run. As more televisions are produced and purchased, they require more electricity to work. As more people are born into the world, greater quantities of fuel are required so that they can cook and keep themselves warm. Yet oil and coal are nonrenewable resources: if and when we exhaust our remaining global reserves of these fuels, how will we light and heat our homes, and run our cars and computers?

Even renewable resources may take many years to be replenished. Hardwood forests, for example, can be obliterated in months but take hundreds of years to regenerate. Yet thousands of acres of these forests are being chopped down annually with little or no attempt to replant them. Food crops, on the other hand, while they can be harvested and replanted each year, still require a certain amount of land. Land—particularly good-quality land—is another limited and increasingly pressured resource. Fish stocks, too, are considered a renewable resource, yet many of the world's edible shoals have now been overfished almost to the point of extinction.

At the same time, many people argue that the world's environment is under increasing strain. Car exhaust fumes, smoke from chimneys, and pollution from factories cause palls of smog to hang for long periods over many large cities. Rivers are widely polluted, and some can no longer support life. Serious problems remain with the disposal of radioactive waste and toxic chemicals. And despite attempts to agree on pollution quotas at the United Nations summits on the environment at Rio de Janeiro, Brazil, in 1992 and Kyoto, Japan, in 1997, greenhouse gases continue to reduce the ozone layer. Global warming is considered by many scientists and concerned citizens to be a serious threat to the future of the planet.

Many experts and commentators contend that the continuing expansion of industry, together with drives for ever-increasing rates of economic growth by governments across the globe, will sooner or later inevitably lead to some form of ecological disaster. Unless, that is, we change our ways. There are vociferous demands for a new, "sustainable" approach to growth and development, one that looks more to recycling waste and resources, and to the preservation and protection of the environment for future generations. More than ever before, a concern for the future of the planet has overtaken the desire to make a fast buck.

Market solutions: magic or myth?

While some governments and businesses broadly support this view (at least in principle), others—particularly some of the larger, more polluting industries, along with some free-market economists and politicians—say that the above arguments are flawed and excessively pessimistic.

Their position is generally that markets will eventually deal with most of the problems outlined above. For example, as resources such as oil and coal begin to run out, prices will rise, so encouraging further exploitation and discovery of new reserves. At the same time, it will become increasingly profitable to develop new technologies and to exploit different forms of energy—solar, wind, and wave power, for example. They predict that more efficient methods of food production will also be developed in order to combat food shortages, while alternatives will be found for hardwood and other similar resources as they become depleted by use. Technologies will be developed to deal with waste, global warming, and so on.

Recent years have certainly seen substantial growth in businesses that specialize in recycling glass, paper, tin, etc., in many parts of the world. There have also been significant advances in the development of alternative sources of energy, with solar panels fitted to houses, and wind turbines now powering parts of some small towns and villages, at least in the developed world. Whether the profit motive alone is a sufficiently strong foundation on which to build ecological awareness remains to be seen. It could be that such developments are too little too late, and a more radical solution to the earth's problems is in fact required.

ABOVE: Wind farms such as this one are increasingly used in the developed world to generate electricity.

Green alternatives

Another important consequence of the massive hike in crude oil prices has been a great increase in research into alternative, renewable sources of energy such as solar power and wind power. As a direct result of this research the cost of power from these sources has fallen significantly. At the present time, however, these renewable energy sources are technically feasible, but they are not yet commercially viable. Nevertheless, economic theory predicts that increases in the price of fossil fuel will lead eventually to a general reliance on renewable alternatives. The day of unreplenishable fossil fuels is drawing to a close—the future would seem to belong to solar power and other alternative sources of energy.

ABOVE: Refuse will be dumped in a particular place and collected only if there is some financial incentive for someone or somebody to deal with it.

Trading the right to pollute

The United States is attacking the problem of acid rain, and its primary weapon in the battle is a transferable permit program. Authorized by the Clean Air Act of 1990, sulfur oxide permits have now been issued by the Environment Protection Agency (EPA) to more than 100 power plants. Sulfur emissions react with water in the atmosphere and fall to earth in the form of acid rain. The goal of the U.S. program is to reduce sulfur emissions from these sources by 10 million tons per year. Each permit allows the emission of one ton of sulfur. The permits are fully transferable, and unused permits may be carried forward to the next year. An interesting aspect of this program is that anyone may purchase permits and retire them—that is, take them out of circulation so that any firm wishing to use them to pollute can no longer do so. This gives environmental groups and private citizens an opportunity to take direct action to improve environmental quality.

Transferable permit programs targeting air quality have also been implemented at the state level. One such program is California's Regional Clean Air Incentives Market (RECLAIM). RECLAIM involves about 400 emitters of air pollutants. The goal of this program is to reduce emissions by 5 to 8 percent each year until 2010.

Source: Tom Tietenberg, "Tradable Permit Approaches to Pollution Control: Faustian Bargain or Paradise Regained?" Department of Economics, Colby College, 1999.

SEE ALSO:

• Volume 3, page 6 Government and the economy

• Volume 3, page 43: Government and business

• Volume 3, page 105: Organizations and boards

• Volume 5, page 36: Externalities, environmental

• Volume 5, page 36: Externalities and government policy

• Volume 5, page 60: Land and natural resources

• Volume 5, page 64: Market failure and anticompetitive practices

ABOVE: Power plants driven by fossil fuels may be replaced by solar- and wind-powered energy sources that are less damaging to the environment.

Glossary

accounts records of earnings, expenditure, assets, and liabilities kept by individuals, firms, and governments.

balance of payments a record of a country's international trade, borrowing, and lending.

balance of trade an indicator of a country's financial condition produced by subtracting the value of imports from the value of exports.

balance sheet a list of assets and liabilities that shows the financial condition of a firm, individual, or other economic unit.

barter a system of trading in which goods are exchanged for other goods rather than for money

black market an illegal part of the economy that is not subject to regulation or taxation and that often deals in high-priced, illegal or scarce commodities.

bond a legal obligation to pay a specified amount of money on a specified future date.

boom and bust a phrase that describes a period of wild swings in economic activity between growth and contraction.

business cycle the periodic but irregular fluctuation in economic activity, usually measured by GDP, which rises and falls for reasons economists do not fully understand.

capital the physical assets owned by a household, firm, or government, such as equipment, real estate, and machinery. Capital is also used to mean financial capital, or money used to finance a business venture.

capitalism an economic system based on private ownership and enterprise and the free market. Capitalism has been the dominant economic system in the western world since around the 16th century.

central bank a public organization, sometimes subject to government influence but often independent, established to oversee and regulate a country's monetary and financial institutions.

commodity a primary product such as coffee, cotton, copper, or rubber. In economics, "commodity" is also used to describe a good or service created by the process of production.

communism a political doctrine based on the ideas of the philosopher Karl Marx that seeks to establish social equality through central regulation of the economic activity and communal ownership. *See also* planned economies.

comparative advantage the advantage gained by a producer—an individual, firm, or government—if they can produce a good at a lower opportunity cost than any other producer.

consumer good an economic good or commodity that is bought for use by a household rather than by industry, for example.

consumer price index (CPI) an economic indicator based on the price of a range of goods and services to calculate an average for expenditure of a U.S. family.

cost benefit analysis the appraisal of a project or policy, for example, by comparing all the social and financial costs with the social and financial benefits arising from that project or policy.

curve a line plotted between points on a graph; an economic curve can be a straight line.

deflation a general downward movement of prices.

demand the desire for a particular good or service backed by the ability to pay for it.

depression a deep trough in the business cycle, usually marked by high prices and high unemployment.

developing country a poor country that is undergoing a process of economic modernization, typically including an increase of GDP through the development of an industrial and commercial base.

economies of scale factors which cause the average cost of producing a good to fall as output increases.

entrepreneurship the ability to perceive opportunities in the market and assemble factors of production to exploit those opportunities.

externality a cost or benefit falling on a third party as the result of an economic activity which is not accounted for by those carrying out that activity.

factors of production the productive resources of an economy, usually defined as land, labor, entrepreneurship, and capital.

fiscal policy the attempts a government makes to maintain economic balance by altering its spending on goods or services or its revenue-raising through taxation.

foreign exchange rate the rate at which one country's money is exchanged for another. The rate is often used as a measure of the relative strengths and weaknesses of different economies.

free trade international trade that is not subject to barriers such as tariffs or quotas.

gross domestic product (GDP) the total value of the final output within the borders of a particular economy.

gross national product (GNP) GDP plus the income accruing to domestic residents from investments abroad, less the income earned in the domestic market by foreigners abroad.

inflation an upward movement in the general level of prices.

interest the amount earned by savers or investors on their deposit or investment or paid by borrowers on their loan. The amount of interest is determined by the interest rate.

Keynesianism an economic doctrine based on the theories of J. M. Keynes that advocates government intervention through fiscal policy to stabilize fluctuations in the economy.

labor the workforce who provide muscle or brainpower for economic activity.

laissez-faire a French term for "let it do," originally used in classic economics to describe an economy with no government intervention.

land land and all natural resources such as oil, timber, and fish.

liquidity a measure of how easily an asset can be converted into cash.

macroeconomics the name given to the study of the economy as a whole rather than with the detailed choices of individuals or firms. *See also* microeconomics.

the market an arrangement which facilitates the buying and selling of a good, service, or factor of production. In a free market the prices which result from this are regulated by the laws of supply and demand rather than by external constraints.

mercantilism an economic policy popular in Europe from the 16th to the 18th centuries that stressed the importance of exports to earn reserves of gold and silver and used high tariffs to prevent imports.

microeconomics the study of individual households and firms, the choices they make in individual markets, and the effects of taxes and government regulation. *See also* macroeconomics.

monetarism an economic doctrine that regards the quantity of money in an economy as the main determinant of aggregate demand. As such, attempts by government to increase output by stimulating demand will only result in inflation.

monetary policy the attempt to regulate inflation and economic activity by varying the money supply and interest rates. Monetary policy is often the responsibility of a central bank.

money supply the amount of liquid assets in an economy that can easily be exchanged for goods and services, usually including notes, coins, and bank deposits that can be transferred by writing checks.

monopoly a market in which there is only one supplier of a good or service for which there is no close substitute.

neocolonialism a relationship between a country and a former colony in which the business interests of the first continue to dominate the economy of the latter.

opportunity cost the best alternative that must be given up when an economic choice is made.

planned economy an economy in which production and distribution are determined by a central authority, such as a ruler or a government.

private sector that part of an economy in which activity is decided and the means of production owned by individuals or firms rather than government. *See also* public sector.

productivity the ratio between the input of resources such as capital and labor and the resulting output of goods and services.

protectionism an economic doctrine that attempts to protect domestic producers by placing tariffs on imported goods.

public sector that part of an economy owned by a government or other public bodies such as state administrations.

recession a severe contraction of economic activity marked by two successive quarters of falling GDP.

specialization the decision by an individual, firm, or government to produce only one or a few goods or services.

sustainable development a form of economic growth that seeks to use renewable rather than finite resources and to minimize the permanent damage done to the environment by economic activity.

supply the quantity of a good or service available for sale at a particular price.

taxes and tariffs compulsory charges placed on economic activity by governments. Taxes might be placed on wealth or income, on business profits, as a sales tax on transactions, or as license fees on activities such as driving. Tariffs are taxes placed on imports into a country.

trusts anticompetitive alliances formed among businesses to force prices up and bring costs down. Trusts were outlawed in the United States by the Sherman Antitrust Act of 1890.

unemployment the condition of adult workers who do not have jobs and are looking for employment.

wealth the total assets of a household, firm, or country less its total liabilities.

welfare state a system of welfare provision by a government to keep its citizens healthy and free from poverty. Welfare provisions typically include free health care, insurance against sickness or unemployment, old age pensions, disability benefits, subsidized housing, and free education.

The World's Economies, 1996

	Population (millions)	GDP $m		Population (millions)	GDP $m		Population (millions)	GDP $m
Afghanistan	20.9	12.8	Germany	81.9	2,364.6	Nigeria	115.0	27.6
Albania	3.4	2.7	Ghana	17.8	6.2	North Korea	22.5	21.5
Algeria	28.8	43.7	Greece	10.5	120.0	Norway	4.3	151.2
Angola	11.2	3.0	Guadeloupe	0.4	3.7	Oman	2.3	15.3
Argentina	35.2	295.1	Guatemala	10.9	16.0	Pakistan	140.0	63.6
Armenia	3.6	2.4	Guinea	7.5	3.8	Panama	2.7	8.2
Australia	18.1	367.8	Guinea-Bissau	1.1	0.3	Papua New Guinea	4.5	5.0
Austria	8.1	226.5	Haiti	7.3	2.3	Paraguay	5.0	9.2
Azerbaijan	7.6	3.6	Honduras	5.8	4.0	Peru	23.9	58.7
Bahamas	0.3	3.5	Hong Kong	6.2	153.3	Philippines	69.3	83.3
Bahrain	0.6	5.7	Hungary	10.0	44.3	Poland	38.6	124.7
Bangladesh	120.1	31.2	Iceland	0.3	7.2	Portugal	9.8	100.9
Barbados	0.3	2.0	India	944.6	357.8	Puerto Rico	3.7	30.3
Belarus	10.3	22.5	Indonesia	200.5	213.4	Qatar	0.6	7.5
Belgium	10.2	268.6	Iran	70.0	132.9	Réunion	0.7	2.9
Benin	5.6	2.0	Iraq	20.6	21.9	Romania	22.7	36.2
Bermuda	0.1	2.1	Ireland	3.6	62.0	Russia	148.1	356.0
Bhutan	1.8	0.3	Israel	5.7	90.3	Rwanda	5.4	1.3
Bolivia	7.6	6.3	Italy	57.2	1,140.5	Saudi Arabia	18.8	125.3
Bosnia	3.6	3.3	Jamaica	2.5	4.1	Senegal	8.5	4.9
Botswana	1.5	4.8	Japan	125.4	5,149.2	Serbia, Montenegro	10.3	15.7
Brazil	161.1	709.6	Jordan	5.6	7.1	Sierra Leone	4.3	0.9
Brunei	0.3	4.6	Kazakhstan	16.8	22.2	Singapore	3.4	93.0
Bulgaria	8.5	9.9	Kenya	27.8	8.7	Slovakia	5.3	18.2
Burkina Faso	10.8	2.4	Kirgizstan	4.5	2.5	Slovenia	1.9	18.4
Burundi	3.2	1.1	Kuwait	1.7	31.0	Somalia	9.8	3.6
Cambodia	10.3	3.1	Laos	5.0	1.9	South Africa	42.4	132.5
Cameroon	13.6	8.4	Latvia	2.5	5.7	South Korea	45.3	483.1
Canada	29.7	569.9	Lebanon	3.1	12.1	Spain	39.7	563.2
Central African			Lesotho	2.1	1.3	Sri Lanka	18.1	13.5
Republic	3.3	1.0	Liberia	2.2	2.3	Sudan	27.3	10.7
Chad	6.5	1.0	Libya	5.6	23.1	Suriname	0.4	1.3
Chile	14.4	70.1	Lithuania	3.7	8.5	Swaziland	0.9	1.1
China	1,232.1	906.1	Luxembourg	0.4	18.9	Sweden	8.8	227.3
Colombia	36.4	80.2	Macau	0.4	7.4	Switzerland	7.2	313.7
Congo	46.8	5.7	Macedonia FYR	2.2	2.0	Syria	14.6	16.8
Congo-Brazzaville	2.7	1.8	Madagascar	15.4	3.4	Taiwan	21.5	275.0
Costa Rica	3.5	9.1	Malawi	9.8	1.8	Tajikistan	5.9	2.0
Cote d'Ivoire	14.0	9.4	Malaysia	20.6	89.8	Tanzania	30.8	5.2
Croatia	4.5	18.1	Mali	11.1	2.4	Thailand	58.7	177.5
Cuba	11.0	18.0	Malta	0.4	3.3	Togo	4.2	1.3
Cyprus	0.8	8.9	Martinique	0.4	3.9	Trinidad and Tobago	1.3	5.0
Czech Republic	10.3	48.9	Mauritania	2.3	1.1	Tunisia	9.2	17.6
Denmark	5.2	168.9	Mauritius	1.1	4.2	Turkey	61.8	177.5
Dominican Republic	8.0	12.8	Mexico	92.7	341.7	Turkmenistan	4.2	4.3
Ecuador	11.7	17.5	Moldova	4.4	2.5	Uganda	20.3	5.8
Egypt	63.3	64.3	Mongolia	2.5	0.9	Ukraine	51.6	60.9
El Salvador	5.8	9.9	Morocco	27.0	34.9	United Arab Emirates	2.3	44.6
Eritrea	3.3	0.8	Mozambique	17.8	1.5	United Kingdom	58.1	1,152.1
Estonia	1.5	4.5	Myanmar	45.9	63.4	United States	269.4	7,433.5
Ethiopia	58.2	6.0	Namibia	1.6	3.6	Uruguay	3.2	18.5
Fiji	0.8	2.0	Nepal	22.0	4.7	Uzbekistan	23.2	23.5
Finland	5.1	119.1	Netherlands	15.6	402.6	Venezuela	22.3	67.3
France	58.3	1,533.6	Netherlands Antilles	0.2	1.9	Vietnam	75.2	21.9
Gabon	1.1	4.4	New Zealand	3.6	57.1	West Bank & Gaza	0.8	3.9
Gambia, The	1.1	0.4	Nicaragua	4.2	1.7	Yemen	15.7	6.0
Georgia	5.4	4.6	Niger	9.5	1.9	Zambia	8.3	3.4
						Zimbabwe	11.4	6.8

Further reading

Allen, L. *Encyclopedia of Money*. Santa Barbara, CA: ABC-Clio, 1999.

Ammer C., and Ammer, D. S. *Dictionary of Business and Economics*. New York: MacMillan Publishing Company, 1986.

Atrill, P. *Accounting and Finance for Non-Specialists*. Engelwood Cliffs, NJ: Prentice Hall, 1997.

Baker, J.C. *International Finance: Management, Markets, and Institutions*. Engelwood Cliffs, NJ: Prentice Hall, 1997.

Baites, B. *Europe and the Third World: From Colonisation to Decolonisation, 1500-1998*. New York: St. Martins Press, 1999.

Bannock, G., Davis, E., and Baxter, R.E. *The Economist Books Dictionary of Economics*. London: Profile Books, 1998.

Barilleaux, R.J. *American Government in Action: Principles, Process, Politics*. Englewood Cliffs, NJ: Prentice Hall, 1995.

Barr, N. *The Economics of the Welfare State*. Stanford, CA: Stanford University Press, 1999.

Barro, R.J. *Macroeconomics*. New York: John Wiley & Sons Inc, 1993.

Baumol, W.J., and Blinder, A.S. *Economics: Principles and Policy*. Forth Worth, TX: Dryden Press, 1998.

Begg, D., Fischer, S., and Dornbusch, R. *Economics*. London: McGraw-Hill, 1997.

Black, J.A. *Dictionary of Economics*. New York: Oxford University Press, 1997.

Blau, F.D., Ferber, M.A., and Winkler, A.E. *The Economics of Women, Men, and Work*. Engelwood Cliffs, NJ: Prentice Hall PTR, 1997.

Boyes, W. and Melvin, M. *Fundamentals of Economics*. Boston, MA: Houghton Mifflin Company, 1999.

Bradley, R.L., Jr. *Oil, Gas, and Government: The U.S. Experience*. Lanham, MD: Rowman and Littlefield, 1996.

Brewer, T.L., and Boyd, G. (ed.). *Globalizing America: the USA in World Integration*. Northampton, MA: Edward Elgar Publishing, 2000.

Brownlee, W.E. *Federal Taxation in America: A Short History*. New York: Cambridge University Press, 1996.

Buchholz, T.G. *From Here to Economy: A Short Cut to Economic Literacy*. New York: Plume, 1996.

Burkett, L., and Temple, T. *Money Matters for Teens Workbook: Age 15-18*. Moody Press, 1998.

Cameron, E. *Early Modern Europe: an Oxford History*. Oxford: Oxford University Press, 1999.

Chown, J.F. *A History of Money: from AD 800*. New York: Routledge, 1996.

Coleman, D.A. *Ecopolitics: Building a Green Society* by Daniel A. Coleman Piscataway, NJ: Rutgers University Press, 1994.

Cornes, R. *The Theory of Externalities, Public Goods, and Club Goods*. New York: Cambridge University Press, 1996.

Dalton, J. *How the Stock Market Works*. New York: Prentice Hall Press, 1993.

Daly, H.E. *Beyond Growth: the Economics of Sustainable Development*. Boston, MA: Beacon Press, 1997.

Dent, H.S., Jr. *The Roaring 2000s: Building the Wealth and Lifestyle you Desire in the Greatest Boom in History*. New York: Simon and Schuster, 1998.

Dicken, P. *Global Shift: Transforming the World Economy*. New York: The Guilford Press, 1998.

Economic Report of the President Transmitted to the Congress. Washington, D.C.: Government Publications Office, 1999.

Elliott, J. H. *The Old World and the New, 1492-1650*. Cambridge: Cambridge University Press, 1992.

Epping, R.C. *A Beginner's Guide to the World Economy*. New York: Vintage Books, 1995.

Ferrell, O.C., and Hirt, G. *Business: A Changing World*. Boston: McGraw Hill College Division, 1999.

Frankel, J.A. *Financial Markets and Monetary Policy*. Cambridge, MA: MIT Press, 1995.

Friedman, D.D. *Hidden Order: The Economics of Everyday Life*. New York: HarperCollins, 1997.

Friedman, M., and Friedman, R. *Free to Choose*. New York: Penguin, 1980.

Glink, I.R. *100 Questions You Should Ask About Your Personal Finances*. New York: Times Books, 1999.

Green, E. *Banking: an Illustrated History*. Oxford: Diane Publishing Co., 1999.

Greer, D.F. *Business, Government, and Society*. Engelwood Cliffs, NJ: Prentice Hall, 1993.

Griffin, R.W., and Ebert, R.J. *Business*. Engelwood Cliffs, NJ: Prentice Hall, 1998.

Hawken, P., et al. *Natural Capitalism: Creating the Next Industrial Revolution*. Boston, MA: Little Brown and Co., 1999.

Hegar, K.W., Pride, W.M., Hughes, R.J., and Kapoor, J. *Business*. Boston: Houghton Mifflin College, 1999.

Heilbroner, R. *The Worldly Philosophers*. New York: Penguin Books, 1991.

Heilbroner, R., and Thurow, L.C. *Economics Explained: Everything You Need to Know About How the Economy Works and Where It's Going*. Touchstone Books, 1998.

Hill, S.D. (ed.). *Consumer Sourcebook*. Detroit, MI: The Gale Group, 1999.

Hirsch, C., Summers, L., and Woods, S.D. *Taxation : Paying for Government*. Austin, TX: Steck-Vaughn Company, 1993.

Houthakker, H.S. *The Economics of Financial Markets*. New York: Oxford University Press, 1996.

Kaufman, H. *Interest Rates, the Markets, and the New Financial World*. New York: Times Books, 1986.

Keynes, J.M. *The General Theory of Employment, Interest, and Money*. New York: Harcourt, Brace, 1936.

Killingsworth, M.R. *Labor Supply*. New York: Cambridge University Press, 1983.

Kosters, M.H. (ed.). *The Effects of Minimum Wage on Employment*. Washington, D.C.: AEI Press, 1996.

Krugman, P.R., and Obstfeld, M. *International Economics: Theory and Policy*. Reading, MA: Addison-Wesley Publishing, 2000.

Landsburg, S.E. *The Armchair Economist: Economics and Everyday Life*. New York: Free Press (Simon and Schuster), 1995.

Lipsey, R.G., Ragan, C.T.S., and Courant, P.N. *Economics*. Reading, MA: Addison Wesley, 1997.

Levine, N. (ed.). *The U.S. and the EU: Economic Relations in a World of Transition*. Lanham, MD: University Press of America, 1996.

MacGregor Burns, J. (ed.). *Government by the People*. Engelwood Cliffs, NJ: Prentice Hall, 1997.

Magnusson, L. *Mercantilism*. New York: Routledge, 1995.

Mayer, T., Duesenberry, J.S., and Aliber, R.Z. *Money, Banking and the Economy*. New York: W.W. Norton and Company, 1996.

Mescon, M.H., Courtland, L.B., and Thill, J.V. *Business Today*. Engelwood Cliffs, NJ: Prentice Hall, 1998.

Morris, K.M, and Siegel, A.M. *The Wall Street Journal Guide to Understanding Personal Finance.* New York: Lightbulb Press Inc, 1997

Naylor, W. Patrick. *10 Steps to Financial Success: a Beginner's Guide to Saving and Investing.* New York: John Wiley & Sons, 1997.

Nelson, B.F., and Stubb, C.G. (ed.) *The European Union : Readings on the Theory and Practice of European Integration.* Boulder, CO: Lynne Rienner Publishers, 1998.

Nicholson, W. *Microeconomic Theory: Basic Principles and Extensions.* Forth Worth, TX: Dryden Press, 1998.

Nordlinger, E.A. *Isolationism Reconfigured: American Foreign Policy for a New Century.* Princeton, NJ: Princeton University Press, 1996.

Painter, D.S. *The Cold War.* New York: Routledge, 1999.

Parkin, M. *Economics.* Reading, MA: Addison-Wesley, 1990.

Parrillo, D.F. *The NASDAQ Handbook.* New York: Probus Publishing, 1992.

Porter, M.E. *On Competition.* Cambridge, MA: Harvard Business School Press, 1998.

Pounds, N.J.G. *An Economic History of Medieval Europe.* Reading, MA: Addison-Wesley, 1994.

Pugh, P., and Garrett, C. *Keynes for Beginners.* Cambridege, U.K.: Icon Books, 1993.

Rima, I.H. *Labor Markets in a Global Economy: An Introduction.* Armonk, NY: M.E. Sharpe, 1996.

Rius *Introducing Marx.* Cambridge, U.K.: Icon Books, 1999.

Rosenberg. J.M. *Dictionary of International Trade.* New York: John Wiley & Sons, 1993.

Rye, D.E. *1,001 Ways to Save, Grow, and Invest Your Money.* Franklin Lakes, NJ: Career Press Inc, 1999.

Rymes, T.K. *The Rise and Fall of Monetarism: The Re-emergence of a Keynesian Monetary Theory and Policy.* Northampton, MA: Edward Elgar Publishing, 1999.

Sachs, J.A., and Larrain, F.B. *Macroeconomics in the Global Economy.* Englewood Cliffs, NJ: Prentice Hall, 1993.

Shapiro, C., and Varian, H.R. *Information Rules: A Strategic Guide to the Network Economy.* Cambridge, MA: Harvard Business School, 1998.

Smith, A. *An Inquiry into the Nature and Causes of the Wealth of Nations,* Edwin Cannan (ed.). Chicago: University of Chicago Press, 1976.

Spulber, N. *The American Economy: the Struggle for Supremacy in the 21st Century.* New York: Cambridge University Press, 1995.

Stubbs, R., and Underhill, G. *Political Economy and the Changing Global Order.* New York: St. Martins Press, 1994.

Teece, D.J. *Economic Performance and the Theory of the Firm.* Northampton, MA: Edward Elgar Publishing, 1998.

Thurow, L.C. *The Future of Capitalism: How Today's Economic Forces Shape Tomorrow's World.* New York: Penguin, USA, 1997.

Tracy, J.A. *Accounting for Dummies.* Foster City, CA: IDG Books Worldwide, 1997.

Tufte, E. R. *Political Control of the Economy.* Princeton, NJ: Princeton University Press, 1978.

Varian, H.R. *Microeconomic Analysis.* New York: W.W. Norton and Company, 1992.

Veblen, T. *The Theory of the Leisure Class (Great Minds Series).* Amherst, NY: Prometheus Books, 1998.

Wallis, J., and Dollery, B. *Market Failure, Government Failure, Leadership and Public Policy.* New York: St. Martin's Press, 1999.

Weaver, C.L. *The Crisis in Social Security: Economic and Political Origins.* Durham, NC: Duke University Press, 1992.

Werner, W., and Smith, S.T. *Wall Street.* New York: Columbia University Press, 1991.

Weygandt, J.J., and Kieso, D.E. (ed.). *Accounting Principles.* New York: John Wiley & Sons Inc, 1996.

Williams, J. (ed.). *Money. A History.* London: British Museum Press, 1997.

Websites

Consumer Product Safety Commission: http://www.cpsc.gov/

Equal Employment Opportunity Commission: http://www.eeoc.gov/

Environmental Protection Agency: http://www.epa.gov/

Federal Reserve System: http://www.federalreserve.gov/

Federal Trade Commission: http://www.ftc.gov/

Food and Drug Administration: http://www.fda.gov/

The Inland Revenue Service: http://www.irs.gov/

Occupational Health and Safety Administration: http://www.osha.gov/

Social Security Administration: http://www.ssa.gov/

The U.S. Chamber of Commerce: http://www.uschamber.com

The U.S. Labor Department: http://www.dol.gov/

The U.S. Treasury Department: http://www.treas.gov/

Picture Credits

Index

125

Fluvanna County High School
1918 Thomas Jefferson Parkway
Palmyra, VA 22963